William Swainson

New Zealand and the War

William Swainson

New Zealand and the War

ISBN/EAN: 9783337014001

Printed in Europe, USA, Canada, Australia, Japan

Cover: Foto ©ninafisch / pixelio.de

More available books at **www.hansebooks.com**

NEW ZEALAND

AND

THE WAR.

BY

WILLIAM SWAINSON, ESQ.,
FORMERLY ATTORNEY-GENERAL FOR NEW ZEALAND,
AUTHOR OF
"NEW ZEALAND AND ITS COLONIZATION," ETC.

LONDON:
SMITH, ELDER AND CO., 65, CORNHILL.

M.DCCC.LXII.

[*The right of Translation is reserved.*]

CONTENTS.

CHAPTER I.

Page

Progress and Prospects of the Colony.—The recent Gold Discovery.—Increase of Population.—The New Zealand Constitution.—New Provinces.—The Church Constitution.—Synodical Action.—" Land Leagues."—The Maori " King Movement."—Policy of Sir George Grey . . 1

CHAPTER II.

State of New Zealand at the time of the Outbreak.—Political *Status* of the Native Race.—Dangerous Consequences of a Collision foreseen.—The Maori Tribal System.—Maori Tenure of Land.—Cause of the Insurrection . . . 45

CHAPTER III.

The Taranaki Settlement.—The Waitara.—The Native Title.—The Waitara considered Essential to the Completeness of the Settlement.—Why valued by its Native Owners.—Their Suspicion of the Settlers.—Their early Determination not to sell the Land 59

CHAPTER IV.

The Government urged to adopt a New System in the Purchase of Native Land.—Declaration of the Governor on the Subject.—Negotiations for the Purchase of the Waitara. — Opposition to the Sale.—Difficulty of completing a Satisfactory Purchase.—A Survey of the Land attempted. — Martial Law proclaimed. — The Land occupied by a Military Force 77

CHAPTER V.

Memorial warning the Governor not to proceed, and showing the Rights of the Native Occupants of the Land.—Rank and Position of William King, the Principal Opponent of the Sale. — Apprehension amongst the Natives excited by the forcible Occupation of the Waitara.—Remonstrances of the Absentee Claimants and others.—Their Petition to the Queen for the Governor's Recal 93

CHAPTER VI.

Question of Title.—Disastrous Consequences to the Taranaki Settlement from the forcible Occupation of the Waitara.—Popularity of the Government Policy.—Debates in the General Assembly.—Sir William Martin's Pamphlet on the " Taranaki Question."—" Notes by the Governor " . 116

CHAPTER VII.

Military Operations.—War risked without Preparation.—Power of the Insurgents underrated.—Repulse of the Troops at Puketekauere.—The Outsettlers driven in.—

Women and Children sent away to the neighbouring Provinces for safety.—The Taranaki Settlements virtually destroyed. — Impracticable Character of the Taranaki Country for Military Operations.—The Insurgents continue to keep the Field.—Embarrassing Position of the Governor.—Sudden Cessation of Hostilities.—Terms of Peace.—Difficulty of Warfare in the Bush.—Cost of the War.—Change in Public Opinion.—Waikato " King Movement."—Change of Ministry.—Sir George Grey appointed Governor.—The Colony saved from a General War 139

CHAPTER VIII.

Impolicy of risking a War at Taranaki.—Policy of the Government as officially explained.—Hostilities: by whom commenced. — The Natives blamed for not appealing to the Law.—Result of the War.—Future Policy 181

NEW ZEALAND.

AND

THE WAR.

CHAPTER I.

Progress and Prospects of the Colony.—The recent Gold Discovery.—Increase of Population.—The New Zealand Constitution.—New Provinces.—The Church Constitution.—Synodical Action.—" Land Leagues."—The Maori " King Movement."—Policy of Sir George Grey.

VARIOUS and valuable as are its known productions, the natural resources of NEW ZEALAND have as yet been very imperfectly developed; but the estimate which was formed of its advantages as a field for British colonization has been verified in almost every particular: and when the confidence of the Natives shall be restored, and when the measures now being taken, under the able administration of Sir George Grey, for establishing peace, order, and government amongst them, shall be completed, New Zealand will assuredly rank as the most attractive and important of our possessions in the Southern Hemisphere.

When the Colony was first founded, neither gold nor wool was counted amongst its probable productions: and the Southern Island was comparatively unknown. But the discovery of a valuable gold-field in the Province of Otago, commencing about thirty or forty miles southward of Dunedin, already promises the most important consequences. In the course of a few weeks 10,000 persons, chiefly from the Australian Colonies, were attracted to the Province, and were engaged in the search for gold. Gold to the value of more than 100,000l. has for some weeks been carried by escort from the ground; in proportion to the numbers employed, the yield largely exceeds the richest of the Victoria gold-fields, and within less than three months the population of the Province was more than doubled.

According to the Official Returns for the year 1860, the English population of New Zealand, amounting to upwards of eighty thousand, was distributed amongst the several Provinces as follows:—

NORTHERN ISLAND.

	English Population.	Maori Population: 1857.
Province of Auckland	23,732	38,269
„ Taranaki	1,239*	3,015
„ Wellington	13,049	8,099
„ Hawkes Bay	2,028	3,673

SOUTHERN ISLAND.

„ Nelson (including Marlborough)	10,178	1,220
„ Canterbury	12,784	638
„ Otago (including Southland)	12,691	525
Stewart Island		200
Chatham Islands		510

But the Colony has now an English population, exclusive of the Native race, of more than 100,000 souls, nearly equally divided between the two Islands; but if the Southern gold-fields shall prove, as they promise to be, not only rich but extensive and permanently productive, the Southern Island will soon have a large preponderance of population; and an attempt will, no doubt, be made to

* A large number of the wives and children of the Taranaki settlers had been temporarily removed from the province in consequence of the war.

have it erected into a separate and independent Colony.

Previous to the recent gold discovery, wool was the great staple product of New Zealand. In the course of seven years the quantity produced has increased sevenfold; and the value of the wool now annually exported from the Colony amounts to more than half a million sterling. It is grown chiefly on the grassy plains of the south; but wool of superior quality is also grown on the cultivated pastures of the Province of Auckland. Sheep-farming, even on the grassy plains and rich pastures of New Zealand, is not without its vicissitudes; but, under the eye of the master, and with ordinary care and attention, it is found to yield a profitable return for the capital employed in it. But nearly the whole of the crown-land available for pastoral purposes is already occupied by a few extensive run-holders, who have for some time been in the receipt of a very considerable income.

A gold-field has for some time been worked in the Province of Nelson which produces a yield of about 50,000*l.* a year. Gold has also been discovered in the Northern Island; and permission has recently been obtained from the Natives to search over the gold-bearing district of the North; and the offer of a free grant of forty acres of land to each immigrant is again, since peace has been restored, attracting to the Province of Auckland a stream of valuable settlers. The other provinces, with the exception of Taranaki, are also making steady progress.

In both Islands the soil and climate have been proved to be adapted to the growth of every description of farm produce. Of the thirty millions of acres of land which have been acquired from the Natives, almost 150,000 acres have been brought into cultivation; and the colonists are already rich in live-stock of every description. More than 15,000 horses, 150,000 head of cattle, and upwards of two millions of sheep, are owned by the settlers alone. The country is liable neither to oppressive heat, severe frost, nor destructive drought; but the climate will disappoint those who expect perpetual sunshine and an atmosphere undisturbed by wind or rain. The weather is changeable, and the seasons are uncertain; but the climate is mild and healthy, and better suited to the English constitution than that of Canada, Australia, or the Cape of Good Hope. For those who are liable to pulmonary disease, there are districts in New Zealand which, as a place of residence, are hardly inferior to Madeira itself, and greatly superior to any part of Italy or the south of France. But in spite of all warning, numbers leave England for the Colonies who are utterly unfitted for a settler's life, not a few of whom find their way to New Zealand; with these exceptions, the settlers who have been steady and industrious have bettered their condition, and the greater number have laid the foundation of an early independence.

The form of Government best suited to the peculiar circumstances of the country is a problem which still remains to be solved. When the subject was under the consideration of Parliament it was obvious that, with its numerous and widely detached settlements, New Zealand could not be governed in detail by a single central authority; and it was provided by the Constitution, that in addition to the general Legislature, six subordinate Provincial Councils should also be established with large powers of legislation. Yet with all this legislative machinery, it was found that there was important districts still governed from a distance, and in which the inhabitants possessed little or no power of local self-government. Three of the most important of these outlying districts have, under the authority of an Act of the Assembly, been recently carved out of the original provinces; and New Zealand is now divided into nine provinces of unequal extent; Auckland, the largest, having an area of upwards of seventeen millions of acres; and the smallest, Taranaki, having an area of between two and three millions only. In some respects the constitution of the three new provinces* differs from that of the provinces established by Parliament: instead of being elected by the people themselves, the Superintendent is chosen by the Council of the province; and an Act passed by any new province cannot come into operation until it shall have received the Governor's assent. But with this restriction, the legislative jurisdiction of the new provinces is equally extensive with that of the original provinces; and there may now be as

* Hawkes Bay, Marlborough, and Southland.

many as 9 different laws in the same country on a variety of important subjects. It still remains to be discovered how the principal settlements, several hundred miles distant from the seat of Government, may have free scope for their development, and how the more thinly-peopled outlying districts may enjoy sufficient power of local self-government, yet in due subordination to a single central authority, and without encumbering the Colony with an inconvenient multiplicity and diversity of laws.

The Natives of New Zealand, like ourselves, appreciate the advantage of law and order; but, like ourselves, they also 'prefer self-government to being governed by a stranger. They say that it is not just that the Maories should be placed entirely in the power of the white man; that salt water and fresh water do not mix well together; and that if their affairs are to be put into the hands of any assembly, they should be placed in the hands of an assembly consisting of their own race. No one would have desired to see the whole of the Natives at once placed on the electoral roll;—but in the first instance, it was generally understood that the Natives, as well as the Colonists, if they were the owners or the individual occupiers of lands or tenements of the value prescribed by the Constitution, would be qualified to vote at the election of Members of the Colonial Legislature; and several of them claimed to be placed upon the electoral roll, and gave their votes at the election, but their claims to vote as owners or occupiers of land held under native tenure was soon called in question. The late Governor's advisers declared the opinion that it is just in itself, and a political necessity, that no electoral qualification should be derived from the tenure or occupation of lands or tenements which are not held under a Crown title; and in pursuance of a Resolution of the House of Representatives, the question was submitted to the Attorney and Solictor-General, whether the Natives can have such possession of any land that is used or occupied by them in common as tribes or communities, and not held under title derived from the Crown, as would qualify them to become electors. The opinion of the Law Officers of the Crown brought to light the fact that the Natives have hitherto been left as entirely without law or tribunal for the determination of questions relating to territorial rights, as they were before the discovery of the country by Captain Cook. "Suppose," say the Law Officers of the Crown, "in a district of Native land lying within the limits of an Electoral District, that one Native by consent of the rest is permitted to have exclusive possession of a piece of land, in which he builds a Native hut for his habitation, but is afterwards turned out or trespassed on by another Native: could he bring an action of ejectment or trespass in the Queen's Court in New Zealand? Does the Queen's Court ever exercise any jurisdiction over real property in a Native district? We presume," they say, "this question must be answered in the negative; and it must of necessity therefore follow that the subjects of householding, occupancy and tenements, and their value in Native districts, are not matters capable of being recognized, ascertained, or regulated by English law." And on the question submitted to them they gave their opinion in the negative. And it has since been admitted by the Colonial Department that the New Zealand Constitution was framed in forgetfulness of the large Native Tribes within the dominions in which it was intended to apply.

If a separation shall take place between the Northern and Southern Islands, the Constitution must of necessity be revised, and an opportunity will be afforded of reconsidering its provisions. But whatever may be its defects, it has proved generally acceptable at least to the English Colonists, and largely instrumental in promoting the progress of the several principal settlements. On leaving the Colony, Governor Browne had the satisfaction of receiving an address from the House of Representatives, assuring him of their appreciation of his endeavours to facilitate the operation of responsible government in the Colony, and to fulfil the promises which he made prior to its introduction. So far also as relates to the Colonists themselves, the experiment of introducing the "responsible" system has been conducted with prudence and moderation. Able men have been found amongst the Colonists to undertake the management of public affairs. The fittest men have hitherto had no difficulty in finding seats in the House of Representatives; and the debates in the Assembly have been conducted with acknowledged ability.

The measures which were prepared by the General Conference for organizing a system of government for the Church in New Zealand have been completed; and though based only on the principle of voluntary compact, they promise to be productive of useful results. If the subject of organizing a constitutional government for the Church of England shall ever become a question of practical importance, something may be learned from the New Zealand experiment. It must be interesting indeed, under any circumstances, to witness the difficulties which churchmen have to encounter when thrown upon their own resources in a new country, without law or organization, without endowments, and beyond the jurisdiction of the ecclesiastical tribunals of the mother country.

Regulations had already been made by the General Conference, prescribing the number of members of which the *first* General Synod should consist; but no provision was made for the constitution of future General Synods; so the first business of the first General Synod, held at Wellington on the 8th of March, 1854, was to prepare a measure for the purpose. And it was provided that in future the General Synod should consist of the several Bishops for the time being; of eighteen Clerical Representatives, to be elected by the clergy; and of twenty-nine Lay Representatives, to be elected by the laity: that every layman of the age of twenty-one years, or upwards, who shall sign a declaration that he is a member of the United Church of England and Ireland, shall be entitled to vote at the election of Lay Representatives for the district in which he may reside; and that every layman, being a communicant and qualified as an elector, shall be qualified to be elected as a Lay Representative.

In addition to a General Synod for the whole Colony, it was provided by the Constitution that a Synod should be established in each diocese; but it remained to be determined what should be the number of the members, their qualification, and the mode of their election; and statutes were passed for the organization of Diocesan Synods and of Archdeaconry Boards; for regulating the formation of parishes; for the appointment of pastors of parishes; for delegating certain of the powers of the General Synod to a standing commission or executive body to act when the Synod itself shall not be in session; and for deciding doubts in the interpretation of the statutes to be passed by the General and the several Diocesan Synods. A measure was also prepared, but left for final consideration at a future session, on the subject of Church discipline;—and after a session extending over a period of twenty-eight days, the first General Synod brought their proceedings to a close. Within less than a year afterwards Synods were also called together in the several dioceses (excepting Waiapu), whose members devoted themselves with considerable zeal and interest to the task of completing the work of organization which the General Synod had begun.

One of the most important of the measures of the first General Synod was the statute to provide for the appointment of pastors to parishes. When it was first mooted, the subject was entirely new to most of the members. As might be expected, opinions were various; and, in the first instance, there was little prospect of unanimity. No ready-made plan was brought forward either by the Bishops, Clergy, or Lay Members. As the discussion proceeded, points of agreement were gradually arrived at. The feeling was unanimous that rights of *private* patronage should not be admitted. No one proposed that the Bishop of the diocese should be the sole and absolute patron; nor, on the other hand, that pastors should be appointed by the parishioners at large. By degrees, the opinion gained ground, that it is important, not to the parish only, but to the Church at large, that a proper appointment should be made to every vacant cure; and that every cure should, if possible, be filled by a clergyman acceptable to the congregation, yet without being directly chosen by themselves, and without being removed from a more extended sphere of usefulness. To secure these objects, it was finally determined that the trust of selecting a clergyman and nominating him to the Bishop of the diocese for institution to a vacant cure, should be vested in a Board of Nominators, to be appointed annually by the Diocesan Synod, and by the Vestry of each parish. But of what number the Board should consist, and in what proportion they should be elected respectively by the Synod and by the Vestry, was left to be determined by the Synod of each diocese.

When the subject afterwards came to be considered by the Synod of the Northern Diocese, the question as to the proportion in which the members of the Board of Nominators should be elected by the Synod and by the parish was debated at considerable length;—a majority of the Lay Members inclining to the opinion that the members of the Board to be elected by the Vestry should exceed the number of members to be elected by the Synod; and it was ultimately determined that the Board of Nominators should consist of five members, two of whom should be elected each year by the Synod, and three by the Vestry of each parish. As not less than two-thirds of the members of the Board must concur in every nomination, no nomination can be made without the concurrence of four out of the five, and consequently no nomination can be made in opposition to the opinion of a majority of the members elected by the Vestry, nor, on the other hand, without the concurrence of one at least of the two members elected by the Synod. As a further safeguard against an improper nomination, the Bishop of the diocese, if not satisfied of the fitness of the party presented by the Board, may reject him; and as a security against the exercise by the Bishop of his power of rejection on arbitrary, frivolous, or vexatious grounds, the rejected nominee may appeal to the House of Bishops, who, if they think the Bishop's alleged grounds of objection insufficient, may over-rule them, and may direct institution to be given. The members are changed every year, so as always to represent the Synod and the Vestry for the time being; but the Board is always in existence, and ready to act whenever a vacancy may occur, special care having been taken that the members of it shall not be elected for the purpose of nominating in any particular case. By means of the members elected by the Vestry, it is expected that the Board will be made acquainted with the condition and circumstances of the parish, and with the views and wishes of the parishioners; and by means of its diocesan members, that the Board will be made acquainted with the character, ability, and antecedents of the several candidates; and that possessing this united knowledge, the Board of Nominators will be qualified to act in the character of a valuable council of advice to the Bishop in appointing the fittest person to the vacant cure. Experience alone can deter-mine the value of the system which has been devised for securing this important object; but the statute passed by the General Synod, supplemented by the Statute of the Diocesan Synod of Auckland for the appointment of a Board of Nominators, may be regarded as affording some test of the fitness of the Colonists for the work they have undertaken of organizing an ecclesiastical system for the Church of England in New Zealand. A Synod is about to be established in the Native Diocese of Waiapu, under the presidency of Bishop Williams; several of the Clerical Members will be Native deacons; the whole of the Lay Representatives will be Natives, and the proceedings will be conducted in the Maori language. Considering the time, the place, and the circumstances, the first meetings of the Synod of the Diocese of Waiapu will be one of the most remarkable events in the history of the Church.

The recent disturbances in the Colony have compelled general attention to the necessity for reconsidering our relations with the Native race.

The Land Leagues which have been formed amongst them, and their connection with the "Maori King Movement," have been frequently misunderstood. In some instances the Natives, in forming a Land League, and in connecting themselves with the King movement, neither intended disloyalty to the Crown, nor wholly to put a veto on the sale of Maori land; their object in placing the land of the Tribe under the care of the King being to make him the arbitrator in case of disputes amongst themselves; to constitute him their mouthpiece as to the land which the tribe as a whole were or were not disposed to sell, so as to prevent the tribal property from being dealt with by individuals, or a fraction only of the Tribe, and thus spare themselves from incessant and destructive feuds. In some cases no doubt the object of the Land League was to maintain their own power and influence by preventing any further alienation of territory; and it can hardly be surprising that a high-spirited people should look with suspicion and misgiving at the increasing numbers and the growing influence of the colonizing race, or that some of their leading Chiefs, seeing a considerable portion of the country already in the hands of the settlers, should have formed an agreement amongst themselves to hold fast to the land which still remains to them.

But unwise as it may be, this compact, so long as it is confined in its operation to those who are parties to it, is no more an offence against the law than an "eight-hours' movement" or a "temperance league," nor is there any reason to fear that it will long be persisted in, or become a practical hindrance to the progress of British colonization. For more than twenty years land has been acquired from the Natives faster than it can be made use of by the Colonists. Nearly the whole of the Middle Island has already become by purchase the property of the Crown; and in the Northern Island, where we have not yet 50,000 Colonists, we have acquired from the Natives seven millions of acres, of which but an insignificant portion has been brought into cultivation. In fact there need be no real difficulty in acquiring the whole of the surplus land of the Natives as fast as we can use it. It is by no means essential to the successful colonization of the country, that the Crown should continue to monopolize the right of purchasing Native land; nor is there any reason why its owners should be virtually compelled to dispose of it at a price below its market value. Let the Government abandon its position as a land dealer. Let all unnecessary restrictions be removed which prevent the Native owner from disposing of his land in open market, and obtaining for it its real value,* and let the Colonists at the same time moderate their apparent eagerness to obtain possession, and the Natives generally will soon become as clamorous to dispose of their land, as some of them have for some time been determined to retain it. But under any circumstances land can always be acquired from the Natives much more quickly, and much more cheaply by fair purchase than by military force. Nor would any true friend dissuade them from parting with their land. Hitherto their rights have been

* "And with regard to the alienation of land, might there not exist a well-founded distrust of a Government which, while it did not permit the sale of land to individuals, does, by holding out inducements which few savages are able to resist, acquire the article which the Maori has to sell at a very low rate (sixpence or a shilling an acre), which article is instantly retailed to the white man at ten shillings an acre!"—*Sir William Denison to Governor Browne.*

recognized and respected, and friendly relations have until recently been maintained between the two races; but if the dominant race, whose flocks and herds are already numbered by the million, shall find themselves cramped for space, and if the progress of colonization shall be seriously impeded, the surplus lands of the Natives will become a bone of contention, with a result which the light of history renders it by no means difficult to foresee.

The attempt has indeed already been made to induce the British Government to regard the conduct of the Natives in resisting what they believed to be an encroachment on their territorial rights, in joining the so-called "King Movement," and in forming a league to retain possession of their lands, as acts of rebellion against the British Crown justifying the confiscation of their land, and calling for the employment of the Queen's Troops at the cost of the Imperial Treasury; but unless the statement officially reported by the late Governor be an unwarrantable libel upon the settlers, that they "are determined to enter in and possess the lands of the Natives, and that neither law nor equity will prevent them," and if it be true, as stated by the late Native Minister, that a degraded portion of the newspaper press had teemed with menaces of this kind, and with scurrilous abuse of the Natives and of all who took an interest in their welfare,—there will always be danger of a Native insurrection, so long as it shall be understood that an extension of territory may be obtained by the forfeiture or confiscation of Native lands. The Native owners of the soil have already peaceably alienated more than half their territory on the most reasonable terms.* Yet although her Majesty has guaranteed

---

* "It might not be generally known that a vast extent of the lands in the Middle Island was obtained from the Natives on certain conditions. The whole of the land commencing at Kaiapoi, and extending south to Molyneux, amounting to about twenty two million of acres, was acquired from the Natives by a payment of 2,000*l.*, and an assurance given by the Commissioner (himself Mr. Mantel), on behalf of the Government, that they must not regard the 2,000*l.* as the principal payment, but the benefits they would acquire from schools erected for their education, from medical attendance, and the general hospitable care of the Government. Those lands passed to the Government, but the promises made had never to this day been properly fulfilled."— *Speech of the Native Minister (Mr. Mantel), House of Representatives.*

Nearly the whole of the land in the Province of Canterbury was purchased from the Natives for little more than a nominal sum; but the land reserved for them (not more than 7,000 acres), is now valued at upwards of 60,000*l.*

to them the undisturbed possession of their land, "so long as it is their wish and desire to retain it," their unwillingness to alienate the land which still remains to them has already been imputed to them as a public offence. If Great Britain would not be again called upon to take part in Native wars, it should be authoritatively declared that while the Imperial Government will be prepared to sanction any measures which may tend to facilitate the acquisition of land in New Zealand for the occupation of our enterprising countrymen, either by direct purchase or otherwise, on equitable terms, they will not under any circumstances acquire or take possession of land in New Zealand by forfeiture, or confiscation, or without the free consent of all who, in accordance with the customs of the country, may be entitled to a voice in the disposal of it; and that they will neither sanction nor permit any violation of that provision of the Treaty of Waitangi which guarantees to her Majesty's Native subjects the possession of their land "so long as it is their wish and desire to retain it." *

* "There is no question that the common and ordinary mode of dealing with the differences between the white man and the Maori would be to treat the latter as a rebel, to pour in troops,

The attempt which has been made by certain of the Tribes to unite themselves under a King, whether for the purpose of maintaining their nationality, for consolidating their power, or of raising themselves from barbarism by means of laws and institutions to be made and administered by themselves, shows a remarkable feature in the character of the race. When the movement for setting up a Maori King first attracted attention, it was viewed by the local authorities not only without apprehension, but as offering, under wise guidance, an opening for good. "If the Government," wrote Governor Browne, "does not take

regardless of expense, and eventually to sweep away a race which occupies land of which the white man professes to be in want, though he has millions of acres of which he can or does make no use. This, however, is a very costly mode of dealing with such a matter; to say nothing of its immorality and injustice.

The Imperial Government will have to pay a high price for the land which, after having purchased it with its blood and treasure, it hands over to the Colonists to sell for their benefit.'—*Sir William Denison to Governor Browne.*

The nature of the territorial rights guaranteed to the Natives by treaty, has been officially defined by the Under Secretary of the Colonial Department (Mr. Merivale), who, in his evidence before a Committee of the House of Commons, declared "that it was considered that the New Zealand Tribes had a right of *proprietorship* over their lands; not simply a general right of dominion, but a right of proprietorship like landlords of estates, for which the Crown was bound to pay them."

the lead and direction of the Native movement into its own hands, the time will pass when it will be possible to do so. * * * The influence of oratory, and, perhaps, evil counsel, aided by the actual excitement of the Natives, may incline them to make laws of their own at these meetings, and thus add to the present difficulty; but they will probably refrain from doing so if they see that the Government is actually doing what they wish." But in the following year (1858), he entertained a different view. "I trust," he said, "that time and absolute indifference and neglect on the part of the Government will teach the Natives the folly of proceedings undertaken only at the promptings of vanity, and instigated by disappointed advisers." * And until a general

---

* When the name of King was afterwards regarded almost as a public offence, the Committee appointed to report upon the finance accounts of the Colony appear to have been surprised to find that the founder of the dynasty, King Potatou, had been in receipt of a pension from the Government almost to the day of his death, and that he had been buried at the cost of the Colonial Treasury. "The Committee observe," says their Report, "that the pension to Te Whero Whero was paid up to the 31st of March, 1860." They are informed that this is the Chief who was proclaimed Maori King under the name of Potatou I., and that he died on the 25th of June, 1860. Out of the item, "Presents and Entertainments to Natives," amounting to 416*l.* 9*s.* 6*d.*,

feeling of apprehension had been excited in the Native mind by the military occupation of the Waitara, the movement had little or no vitality which, by prudent guidance, might not have been turned to valuable account.

According to the Report of the Waikato Committee, the object of a large section of the Natives was distinctly expressed at a great meeting in the Waikato, in April, 1857, at which the Governor was present, and at which it was understood by them that his Excellency promised to introduce amongst them institutions of law, founded on the principle of self-government, analogous to British institutions, and presided over by the British Government. "I was present," says the Rev. Mr. Ashwell, referring to that meeting, "when Te Wharepu, Paehia, with Potatou, asked the Governor for a Magistrate, Laws, and Runangas, which he assented to; and some of the Natives took off their hats and cried, "Hurrah!"" "I want order and laws," were, in fact, the first words of the leading member of the movement for

the Committee discovered that the sum of 1*l*. 17*s*. was paid on the 11th of November, 1860, *for coffin furniture* for Potatou. " The facts and dates," adds the Report, "appeared to the Committee to be very remarkable."

establishing a Maori King. "The King would give us these better than the Governor, for the Governor has never done anything, except when a *Pakeha* was killed; he lets us kill each other and fight. A King would stop these evils."

The two most active leaders of the movement may be taken as representative men of the new generation of Maori Chiefs. William Thompson is remarkably silent and reserved; he listens patiently to what is said, but thinks and decides for himself. He spends a great part of his time in writing; noting down everything remarkable he sees, hears, or reads; and he is engaged in constant correspondence with all parts of the country. He is well versed in Scripture History; —a fluent speaker and a formidable antagonist in debate. Though he is the son of a celebrated warrior, he prides himself on his character as a peacemaker. When several hundred armed Natives descended the Waikato River, in a state of dangerous excitement, to inquire into the violent death of one of their countrymen in the neighbourhood of Auckland, he himself formed one of the party for the purpose of restraining them, and he was largely influential in keeping them from mischief. Several unruly and headstrong members of his Tribe went to Taranaki to the support of William King, but it was without his sanction or authority; and he himself afterwards proceeded to the seat of war, and succeeded, though not without great difficulty, in withdrawing them, and in bringing about a general cessation of hostilities.

"I thought," he said, describing his own share in the movement, "about building a large house as a house of meeting for the Tribes who were living at variance in New Zealand, and who would not become united. That house was erected, and was called Babel. I then sent my thoughts to seek some plan by which the Maori Tribes should become united, that they should assemble together and the people become one, like the Pakehas. * * * Evil still manifested itself; the river of blood was not yet stopped. The ministers acted bravely, and so did I, but the flow of blood did not cease. When you came, the river of blood was still open, and I therefore sought for some thought to cause it to cease, as the ministers had long persevered. I considered how this blood could be made to diminish in this Island. I looked into your books where Israel cried to have a King for themselves, to be a judge over them, and I looked at the words of Moses in Deuteronomy xvii. 15, and in 1 Samuel viii. 4, and I kept these words in my memory through all the years;—the land feuds continuing all the time, and blood still being spilt, I still meditating upon the matters, when we arrived at the year 1857. Te Heuheu called a meeting at Taupo. Twice 800 were assembled there, when the news of that meeting reached me. I said, I will consent to this, to assist my work, that the religion of those Tribes that had not yet united might have time to breathe. I commenced at those words in the Book of Samuel viii. 5: 'Give us a King to judge us.' This was why I set up Potatau in the year 1857. On his being set up, the blood at once ceased, and has so remained up to the present year. The reason why I set up Potatau as a King for me was, he was a man of extended influence, and one who was respected by the Tribes of this Island. That, O friend! was why I set him up; to put down my troubles, to hold the land of the slave, and to judge the offences of the chiefs. The King was set up; the Runangas were set up; the Kai-whakawas were set up, and religion was set up. The works of my ancestors have ceased, they are diminishing at the present time; what I say is, that the blood of the Maories has ceased to flow. I don't allude to this blood (lately shed). It was your hasty work caused that blood. I do not desire to cast the Queen from this Island, but from my piece of land. I am to be the person to overlook my piece."

A similar account of the origin of the movement was given by Renata, another of its earliest and most influential supporters. After passing sometime in captivity in the North, where he received (in 1842-3) some teaching at the Waimate school, Renata returned to his own people in the Hawkes Bay district, where both with the settlers and the Natives he has established a high character for his ability and integrity. For several years he has been engaged in promoting the building of Native churches, schools, and flour-mills; for some time he employed at his own cost an English teacher to instruct the Native children. "It was my wrongs unredressed by you," he said, "that induced me to set about to work out an idea of my own; that is, Waikato, the tribe who set it going. They were in doubt whether to term Chief or Governor, and neither suited, and they established him as 'the Maori King;' it was tried experimentally, and proved as a means of redress for wrongs not settled by you, by the Government. The only wrongs you redressed were those against yourselves; but as for those all over the breadth of the country, you left them unnoticed. Sir, the enemies he (the Maori King) had to fight with were the crimes of the Maori; his murders, his thefts, his adulteries, his drunkenness, his selling land by stealth. These were what he had to deal with. * * * Did I set up any King in secret? As I view it, Waikato wished that his authority should emanate from the Governor. And then it was that we tried to do the best we could for ourselves. When it was seen that evil was partly put down by the Runanga, and the stupid drunkards became men once more, then the work (the King movement) became general.

"But is this (King movement) indeed to cause a division between us? No, it will be caused by secret purchases of land, the thing which has been going on for years." And Renata was careful to make it clear that the promoters of the movement had no intention to subvert the Queen's authority. "You say, 'The Maories are not able to fight against the Queen of England, and kill (prevail against) her.' This is my answer. Sir, you know perfectly well that the Maori will be beaten; though it be said that this war is for sovereignty, the fault of the Governor can never be concealed by that. Who is the Maori that is such a fool as to be mistaken about the sovereignty or supremacy of the Queen of England? Or who will throw himself away in fighting for such a cause? No, it is for land; for land has been the prime cause of war amongst the Maories from time immemorial down to the arrival of Pakehas in this island of ours. The Maori will not be daunted by his weakness, by his inferiority, or the smallness of his Tribe; he sees his land going, and will he sit still? No; but he will take himself off (to resist). The Queen's sovereignty has been acknowledged long ago: had it been to fight for supremacy, probably every man in this island would have been up in arms; but in the present case the fighting is confined to the land which is being taken possession of. There is a letter of William King's lying here, in which he says that if his land is evacuated, he will put a stop to the fighting. * * * * It was proposed to leave it to the Queen to judge between the Governor and William King: you witnessed the general assent of all to that proposal that the Queen should be the judge. Well, does this look in your opinion like a rebellious word in regard to the Queen, that you have left it out of sight, and taken up that word of your own invention about the Maori making war against the Queen? Sir, the Maori does not consider that he is fighting against the Queen; I beg therefore that you will cease to pervert words, and rather consent to our proposal that we should all join in writing a letter to the Governor (to propose) that the war may be stopped, and that it may be left for the Queen to decide in this quarrel; and then let us write a letter to the Queen (to pray) that she will send a Commissioner (Kainhakawa) to stand between us, and let us all join together in inquiring into this dispute. Cease (arbitration) by guns, and now let it be left to inquiry, that a remnant of men be left."

After a careful inquiry into the subject, a Committee of the House of Representatives, comprising several of its leading members, reported their opinion (1860) that a great movement had been going on amongst the Native people, having for its main object the establishment of some settled authority amongst themselves; that such movement need not have been the subject of alarm; that its objects were not necessarily inconsistent with the recognition of the Queen's supreme authority, or with the progress of colonization; and that it would have been from the first, and would then be, unwise to contradict it by positive resistance—an opinion which has been confirmed by the leader of the present Ministry. " The great national movement," said Mr. Fox, "which has been seething in the Native mind for years past, is not, as the Duke of Newcastle has been taught to think it, based on a desire to get rid of British rule and British civilization; but we recognize in it the desire of the Native race for self-elevation: we see in it an earnest longing for law and order, and an attempt (not feeble or ill-directed had it only been encouraged and guided,) to rise to a social equality with ourselves;" and there is no doubt that if judiciously dealt with, this remarkable movement might have been turned to valuable account, and that few of the Chiefs who ever formally acknowledged the sovereignty of the Crown would ever have desired to establish a national independence.

After the admission made by the Colonial Minister,* "that without the control of larger funds for Native purposes than have been placed at the disposal of the Governor, it has been impossible to adopt such measures as would be effectual for the Government and civilization of the Maories," and after the admission of the Colonial Under-Secretary,† that "the Governor of New Zealand is obliged to act under a Constitution which appears to have been framed in forgetfulness of the large Native Tribes within the dominions to which it was intended to apply," it is hardly surprising that an attempt should be made by the New Zealanders to find out some mode of government for themselves in their relations with each other. More than twenty years ago, the British Government, in assuming

* The Duke of Newcastle.   † Mr. Fortescue.

the sovereignty, undertook the responsibility of establishing law and order in the country. Yet the late Governor has declared that our Government in many places is almost unknown by the Natives;—that some of the most populous districts—such as Hokianga and Kaipara—have no magistrates resident among them; and many —such as Taupo, the Ngatiruanui, Taranaki, and the country about the East Cape—have never been visited by an officer of the Government. " The residents in these districts have never felt that they are the subjects of the Queen of England, and have little reason to think that the Government of the Colony cares at all about their welfare." And yet, by the treaty of Waitangi, the Maori people were guaranteed all the rights and privileges of British subjects; but though they are taxed as subjects, they are not allowed to take part in making laws even for the Government of their own people; in matters of a criminal nature, even when a Maori is concerned, they are allowed to take no part in the administration of the law; and neither by the English laws, nor by laws specially made for them, has her Majesty's sovereignty been exercised to promote peace, order, or law amongst the great bulk of the Maori people.* And until recently little or nothing has been done or attempted to take advantage of the desire of the Natives for law, and of their aptitude for self-government. But with the new Ministry, and under the administration of Sir George Grey, there is ground to hope that measures will be taken for establishing law and order amongst them on a sound and permanent footing. "The first great principle," said Mr. Fox, in his exposition of the policy of the new

* "You have, now, as a fact, the establishment of something analogous to a general government among the Maories; a recognition on their part of the necessity of some paramount authority; this is a step in the right direction—do not ignore it—do not, on the ground that some evil may possibly spring from it, make the Natives suspicious of your motive by opposing it, but avail yourself of the opportunity to introduce some more of the elements of good government among them. Suggest to them the necessity of defining and limiting the power of the person who has been elected as the Chief or King (I should not quarrel with the name); of establishing some system of legislation, simple, of course, at first, but capable of being modified and improved; but do not attempt to introduce the complicated arrangements suited to a civilized and educated people, recognizing publicly and openly the Maories not merely as individual subjects of the Queen, but as a race—a body whose interests you are bound to respect and promote, and then give to that body the means of deciding what their interests are, and of submitting them in a proper form for your consideration."—*Sir William Denison to Governor Browne.*

Government, "on which we base our policy is this, that the Maories are men of like passions and feelings, and to be acted on by the same motives, as ourselves. It may seem strange to be standing up to assert that the Natives are men. But it is necessary to assert it, for the theory of the Native Office and its practice have been to treat them, not as men, but as spoiled children. It is necessary also to assert that they are of like passions, and to be operated on by like motives, as ourselves; for there are those in this House, and out of it, who see in the dark skins of the Natives a warrant for dealing with them on principles different altogether from those on which we should deal with each other, who believe that because the New Zealander came from Asia, he must be governed differently from the Saxon race. * * * I do not hesitate to say that of all the races on the face of the earth, there is none that comes so near to the Anglo-Saxon in temperament, in mental capacity, and in habit of thought, as the Maori." After failing to fulfil our own obligations, to attempt, by brute force, to stifle the instinctive yearning of a brave people for the preservation of their nationality, and for the introduction of order and law, would be a reproach to civilization, and a disgrace to British rule.

Any fusion of the two races, however, into one system of government, it has been said, is not at present possible. The establishment of separate institutions for the Native race is the only alternative; and this is the very thing which they crave at our hands. And the measures which Sir George Grey is now engaged in bringing into operation are based upon the principle that the Maories themselves should, as far as practicable, make and enforce regulations suited to their own requirements, and have a share in the administration of the government of their own country. It is proposed that the Native territory shall be divided into convenient districts, for the purpose of local self-government, that in each district there shall be an English Civil Commissioner, a Runanga or Native Council, consisting of the leading men of the district, who are to be paid, and to act also as Magistrates or Assessors; a small body of Native Police, an English medical man, and a Native clergyman, to act also as schoolmaster. The District Council is to be presided over by the Civil Commissioner, and to have the power of preparing bye-laws, to be brought into operation with the approval of the Governor in Council, on the subjects of fencing, cattle trespassing, the suppression of nuisances, for regulating the sale of spirits, &c., and other subjects prescribed by an Act passed some time ago by the General Assembly. It is intended that the Council shall also have the power of inspecting schools, erecting gaols and hospitals, and constructing roads (not being main lines of road) within the districts; of deciding who may be the true owners of any Native lands within the districts, and of recommending the terms and conditions on which Crown grants may be issued to tribes, families, or individuals.

It is also intended that the Civil Commissioner, resident Magistrates and Native Assessors shall periodically hold Courts within the district, and that in all cases in which the punishment awarded shall exceed a certain amount, their proceedings shall be submitted for review to a Judge of the Supreme Court: that Native offenders, instead of being taken to the gaols in the English settlements, shall be confined in the district prison, and tried by a jury of their countrymen in their own district and by a Judge of the Supreme Court on circuit.

It forms, also, an important feature in Sir George Grey's scheme of Native policy, to relax the restrictions by which the Natives have hitherto been prevented from disposing of their lands, excepting to the Crown; and when the boundaries and ownership of land in any district shall have been ascertained in accordance with the regulations of the Native Council, the Native owners will be allowed to dispose of it by direct sale to any purchaser who may be approved of by the Government on the recommendation of the Council, on such conditions as may be agreed on between the sellers and the purchaser. The intending purchaser, however, must be a *bonâ fide* settler, and will not be entitled to a Crown grant of the land until he shall have been in personal occupation for at least three years. It is also intended that the Native owners shall be permitted to lease such lands upon terms to be decided on by the Government on consultation with the Council of the district. A lost confidence is not easily regained, but, by these means, Governor Grey is endeavouring to remove the causes of suspicion and irritation which exist amongst the Native people, in the expectation that before the proved and substantial benefits of the Queen's sovereignty the "King Movement" will die out. "In this way, the Government will have discharged its duty to this people: it will have become, for the first time, the Government of the Maori as well as of the Pakeha: and will have saved the Colony from the misery, and the mother country from the burden, of a protracted and costly war." *

* An official notification recently published amongst the Natives concludes as follows: (Translated:—) "This, then, is what the Governor intends to do, to assist the Maori in the good work of establishing law and order. These are the first things:—the Runangas, the Assessors, the Policemen, the Schools, the Doctors, the Civil Commissioners to assist the Maories to govern themselves, to make good laws, and to protect the weak against the strong. There will be many more things to be planned and to be decided; but about such things the Runangas and the Commissioners will consult. This work will be a work of time, like the growing of a large tree—at first there is the seed, then there is one trunk, then there are branches innumerable, and very many leaves: by-and-by, perhaps, there will be fruit also. But the growth of the tree is slow—the branches, the leaves, and fruit did not appear all at once, when the seed was put in the ground: and so will it be with the good laws of the Runanga. This is the seed which the Governor desires to sow:—the Runangas, the Assessors, the Commissioners, and the rest. By-and-by, perhaps, this seed will grow into a very great tree, which will bear good fruit on all its branches. The Maories, then, must assist in the planting of this tree, in the training of its branches, in cultivating the ground about its roots; and, as the tree grows, the children of the Maori, also, will grow to be a rich, wise, and prosperous people, like the English and those other nations which long ago began the work of making good laws, and obeying them. This will be the work of peace, on which the blessing of Providence will rest,—which will make the storms to pass away from the sky,—and all things become light between the Maori and the Pakeha; and the heart of the Queen will then be glad when she hears that the two races are living quietly together, as brothers, in the good and prosperous land of New Zealand."

CHAPTER II.

State of New Zealand at the time of the Outbreak.—Political *Status* of the Native Race.—Dangerous Consequences of a Collision foreseen.—The Maori Tribal System.—Maori Tenure of Land.—Cause of the Insurrection.

OUR former wars with the Natives of New Zealand were almost inevitable; but they left no rankling feeling in the Native mind: and not only our gracious Sovereign, but the various Representatives of her Majesty* have, up to a

* The Governor is commonly, but erroneously regarded as the "Representative" of the Crown. "Not in fact," says Lord Brougham; "he does not even represent the Sovereign *generally*, having only the functions delegated to him by his Commission; and being only the officer to execute the special powers with which the Commission clothes him." And the Maories have always been taught by authority to regard the Queen personally as their ruler and governor, who, though far away, is ever mindful of their interests; and to whom, if wronged, they are to appeal as one ever willing to listen to their words.

Letter of Governor Grey to Te Whero Whero, dated 31st of October, 1858.

[After stating the gracious answer of the Queen to the memorial addressed to her by the Chiefs of Waikato, the Governor proceeds to say:—]

recent period, enjoyed the respect and confidence of the Maori race. Queen Victoria is still believed by them to be the loving mother of her Native subjects; but recently, and for the first time in the history of the Colony, many of them, for a time at least, became dissatisfied with our rule.

Before the commencement of the Taranaki insurrection, New Zealand was in a state of profound peace. For a period of several years, friendly relations had been maintained between the settlers and the Natives, and the Colony had been making steady progress in agriculture,

" *My good Friends*—These are the words of the Queen to you. I add a few words of my own. Listen to them. You thought trouble was coming upon you, so you wrote your loving thoughts to the Queen, and disclosed your fear to her. The Queen was not deaf to your appeal, but attended to it immediately; and quickly came her letter to remove your anxiety. Quite full is her letter of words of love and kindness, in return for your love to her.

"Learn from this, that though the Queen is far away, yet her love is nigh, and reaches you speedily. Her mindfulness of you is near at hand to protect you. If you shall think hereafter that you are trampled on by any person whomsoever—be patient. Let not the heart in its ignorance be excited and led by wrath into wrong. On the contrary, write your thoughts to the Queen, for you see her willingness to listen to your words.

"From your loving friend,
"G. GREY
"*Governor-in-Chief.*"

commerce, population, and wealth. Upwards of thirty millions of acres—more than half the area of the whole of the islands—had been obtained from the Native owners, for purposes of colonization; internal feuds had almost ceased; a growing desire for the establishment of law and order amongst themselves was showing itself amongst the Natives in all parts of the country: and with wise government and prudent conduct on the part of the settlers, there appeared to be a fair prospect of uninterrupted prosperity and peace.

For several years after the Colony was founded, the Governor was advised by a Council appointed by and responsible to the Crown, and who held their offices by a permanent tenure: but his advisers are now responsible to the Colonists alone, and are liable to be frequently changed. When this important alteration in the form of Government was effected, it was proposed by the Governor that, as to Native affairs, both power and responsibility should continue with the Governor as before, but that the Ministers should have the right of tendering their advice. The risk of weakening the Governor's power, and of exposing him to be influenced by the varying and irresponsible counsels of successive Administrations holding office at the popular will, was regarded by many as a serious danger; and it was foretold that the Chiefs, if neglected by the Head of the Government, and left to be dealt with by subordinates, would gradually secede from communication with the authorities, forming leagues and schemes of which the Government would have no cognizance: that they would thus become estranged, and that when they came to be feared and suspected, there would be the constant risk of the Governor being driven by the Ministers to use the Troops against them; and that the country would not be safe for six months after the question of peace and war had been entrusted to a Ministry who had the command of the Queen's Troops, but who were themselves neither responsible to the Colonists nor to the Crown.

In terms, at least, the New Zealand Constitution makes no distinction of race. The Natives are acknowledged to be the owners of the soil—to have, in fact, a right of proprietorship like landlords of estates; but it has been denied that they have such an interest in it under the Native tenure as to entitle them, within the meaning of the Act, to vote at the election. In return for their cession of the sovereignty, we have undertaken to impart to them the rights and privileges of British subjects. Yet we have given them no voice in the Government of the country, while we tax them for its support. They are not entitled by law to act as jurors: and they are not tried by a jury of their peers if they offend against the law. Though acknowledged to be the owners of the soil, we have given them no constitutional tribunal by which conflicting claims to land may be judicially determined. If a Colonist resists a threatened injury to his person, or his property, he exercises a right common to every English subject of the Crown; but when the Maories, to whom we have covenanted to impart these rights, attempted to assert and maintain them, they were denounced as rebels, and immediately subjected to the authority of military law. When it was urged in their behalf that before being subjected to martial law, they were entitled to have their claims considered and determined by the civil tribunals of the country, a doubt was raised whether they are so far British subjects as to be entitled to the rights and privileges of a subject of the Crown; and those who attempted to aid them in obtaining justice were charged with disloyalty to the Sovereign, and their interference was declared by those who were then in authority to amount to a public danger. We are more scrupulous than the French in our professions of regard for the rights of the coloured races who may be subject to our rule; but we have given our French neighbours some ground to maintain that the difference between their system of colonization and our own, is in truth more theoretical than real.

But the colonization of these Islands having been undertaken on the avowed principle that the rights of the Aborigines shall be carefully respected, the project has always been regarded as an experiment in which the national credit was at stake. The first Governor was instructed that the Native inhabitants should be the objects of his constant solicitude; that there was no subject connected with New Zealand which the Queen, and every class of her Majesty's subjects, regarded with more earnest anxiety; that the dread of exposing any part of the human race to the dangers which had commonly proved so formidable to Native tribes when brought into contact with civilized men, was the motive which for a length of time dissuaded the occupation of New Zealand by the British Government; and it was enjoined upon the first Governor, that amongst the principal objects to be aimed at by him, was the protection of her Majesty's Native subjects from cruelty and wrong; the establishment and maintenance of friendly relations with them; and the prevention of the diminution of their numbers; and that to save them from the calamities of which the approach of civilized men to barbarous tribes had been the almost universal herald was a duty too serious and important to be neglected. Having been engaged for upwards of twenty years in this great experiment, and not without some prospect of success, it is humiliating to have to record that a number of her Majesty's Maori subjects took up arms to defend themselves from what they believed to be the injustice of their rulers; and that a demand was understood to have been made upon Great Britain by the Colonial Native Minister for an "indefinite expenditure of blood and treasure," in order to subdue them.

The late Governor had not been many months in the Colony before he discovered, and, like his predecessors, pointed out the danger of provoking a conflict with the Natives. "In any real trial of strength between the Natives and Europeans there can be no possible doubt," reported Governor Browne, "as to the result. But it is not less certain that pending its duration a· vast amount of life and property would be destroyed: numbers of thriving settlers would abandon their houses: immigration would entirely cease; and a great expense would be entailed on the mother country. In other words," he added, "the prosperity of the Colony would be annihilated for years after the termination of a struggle as successful as could be desired." It had been declared also by one of the numerous writers on New Zealand, referring especially to that part of the country which became the seat of war, that the land might have been wrested from the Natives, but that fighting, however successful, must have been attended with some deplorable result. The Natives might have been driven off, but their revengful feelings thus excited, who, in a scattered agricultural community like this, was to ensure the remote settlers against the attack of some marauding band? Certainly not the soldiers. "Peaceful purchase, on the contrary," the writer adds, "is attended with many excellent results." Six years previously the then Native Secretary had recorded his opinion, "that military operations in the Taranaki district would prove fatal to the prosperity of the settlement for some time to come, as the settlers would have to concentrate themselves in town, for the protection of their wives and families, and their properties in the meantime would go to ruin." And more recently, the late Governor had informed the Colonial Minister, "that the immediate consequences of any attempt to acquire Maori lands, without previously extinguishing the Native title to the satisfaction of all having an immediate interest in them, would be an universal outbreak, in which many innocent Europeans would perish, and colonization would be indefinitely retarded." Yet after having acquired more than thirty millions of acres of land under a system satisfactory, in the main, both to the buyer and the sellers, a "new policy" was believed by the

Natives to have been attempted, and the Province of Taranaki was plunged into a civil war, by an attempt to obtain possession, by military force, of Native land with a doubtful or disputed title.

When we first became acquainted with New Zealand, the whole country from the North Cape to Stewart's Island was parcelled out by natural or other well-known landmarks amongst the numerous tribes and families who form the Maori race. Each community holds its land in common; but every individual member, besides having a general interest in the Tribal property, may acquire by inheritance, by his own labour, or otherwise, a possessory or holding title to a specific portion, but he is not allowed to exercise a disposing power over it. "It is right," said an intelligent Chief, "that every individual should be free to sell his own bushel of wheat, potatoes, and corn, for they are produced by the labour of his hands; but the land is an inheritance from our ancestors,—the Father of us all." And so general is the Tribal system, that in the opinion of the Head of the Native Department (1856), "no Native can claim an individual title to land in the Northern Island. There is really no such thing as individual title that is not entangled with the general interest of the Tribe; and often with the claims of other Tribes, who may have emigrated from the locality."

The common property is, in fact, the bond which binds together the members of the Tribe; and it would be inconsistent with the Tribal system if an individual could alienate away from the Tribe any portion of territory; for all the members have not only a present right in the uncultivated or unappropriated land, but also a reversionary interest in those portions of the land which have already been appropriated by other members of the Tribe; and it would be fatal not only to the Tribal system, but to the existence of the Tribe itself, if individuals had the power of their own free will of alienating to a stranger any portion of the common land. Nor does the Chief himself hold land on any different tenure. In addition to a general interest in the common property, he has frequently, like some of the ordinary members of the Tribe, a possessory or holding title to some specific portion of it; but he is not recognized as having the power at his own individual will of separating it from the common stock, and selling it to a stranger. From his superior ability and position, he exercises a powerful influence over their deliberations: he has also an influential voice as to the sale or disposal of the common land: yet if all were desirous that a portion of it should be sold, he would hardly have the power by virtue of his Chieftainship to put an absolute veto on the sale: nor could he, on the other hand, without the consent of the Tribe, undertake to dispose of any portion of the Tribal land; his duty being to act as the guardian of the common property, and to give expression to the common will.

Early in the year 1860 an attempt to purchase land without obtaining the consent of all those who claimed to be entitled to a voice in the disposal of it, provoked the Natives of Taranaki to take up arms in defence of their territorial rights, and led to a formidable insurrection. Some years previously, a somewhat similar proceeding on the part of the American Government excited the apprehension of the Red Indians, who also held their lands in common. "In the year 1825 the United States Government," says the Abbé Domenech,* " wishing to satisfy the State of

* *Seven Years' Residence*, &c.

Georgia, resolved to take possession of a large portion of land still occupied by the Creeks. McIntosh and a few other members of the nation leaned towards the concession, but the great majority would not hear of it. The Commissaries of the Georgian Legislature, knowing the state of feeling, hastily called an assembly of Chiefs on a spot named Indian Spring. In this important reunion one of the Chiefs arose, and addressing the Commissaries, said: 'We have already seen you at the Broken Arrow, and told you that we have no land to sell. Then, as now, I have heard no complaints against my nation. Called forth in haste, we have come to meet you, but do not consider the Chiefs here present as having authority to treat with you. McIntosh knows we are tied down by our laws, and that which is not resolved on in our public places, by our General Councils, does not bind the nation. I am obliged to repeat to you what I said to you at the Broken Arrow, we have no land to sell. There are here few members of our upper towns, and many of those of the lower towns are absent. McIntosh knows that no portion of land can be sold without a Grand Council, and without the unanimous consent of the whole nation; and that if a part of the people wish to leave, they may go, but cannot sell their land, which in that case belongs to the nation. This is all I had to say to you, and now I return home.' The Commissaries did not, however, give up the game: they told McIntosh and his companions that the Creeks were sufficiently represented by them, and the idea of dividing among them the money that Government destined for the purchase, led the Indians to conclude with the Commissaries. Nineteen Chiefs only signed the concession; the others, more or less, however, were of inferior rank, and contemptible characters. Thirty-six refused to sign. This treaty of the Indian Spring," continues the Abbé Domenech, " spread uneasiness on every side."

CHAPTER III.

The Taranaki Settlement.—The Waitara.—The Native Title.—The Waitara considered essential to the Completeness of the Settlement.—Why valued by its Native Owners.—Their Suspicion of the Settlers.—Their early determination not to sell the Land.

THE Province in which the outbreak occurred is the smallest of the nine Provinces into which the Colony has been divided: but " no one can speak of the soil or scenery of New Zealand, till he has seen both the natural beauties and the ripening harvests of Taranaki, which by concurrent testimony is described as the garden of New Zealand." From the beginning of March, 1860, to the end of March in the following year, this beautiful district was visited by the scourge of war. Its once fruitful fields and pleasant homesteads were abandoned and laid waste; the ploughshare was exchanged for the sword; and the settlers, separated from their wives and families, and shut up in an entrenched camp, within sight of the wasted labours of nearly twenty years, were for many months doing military duty under the iron despotism of martial law.

With a seaboard of about 100 miles, of which Cape Egmont is the centre, the Province extends inland from twenty to forty miles; and it comprises an area of about two millions of acres. With the exception of a narrow and irregular strip of open fern-land near the sea, the country is heavily timbered. At the commencement of the outbreak, the English population of the province amounted to 2,700 souls; and the Native population was estimated to amount to about an equal number. But not having a harbour, being difficult of access, hemmed in between an open roadstead and a dense forest, and being almost impracticable for military operations, the Taranaki district, where the question of Native title has always been unusually complicated, was not well chosen, with all its natural beauties, for the site of an English settlement.

The New Zealand Company, acting with their usual precipitancy, and ignorant as to who were the real owners of the land, dealt with a few Natives who represented themselves to have the right to dispose of it, and hardly made the shadow of a purchase before the settlement was founded. The first difficulty with which the early settlers had to contend, as at Wellington and Nelson, was the want of a clear title to the land; and it was only by the exertions of the Government that the Native title to a few blocks of land of limited extent was afterwards extinguished, and the settlers, after a period of ruinous delay, were ultimately put into peaceable possession of their homesteads.

The Waitara, a fertile, open district, watered by a small river, ten miles to the north of the town, and navigable at high water by small coasting craft, was the locality which in the first instance was fixed upon for the site of the settlement; and it was represented by their surveyer to the New Plymouth Company, by whom the settlement was originally founded, that if they were deprived of that river, they would lose the only harbour in the neighbourhood, and the most valuable district for agriculture. But this much coveted spot was not to be obtained from its Native owners; so the Company were compelled with great reluctance to lay out the town upon a much less eligible site;

and for nearly twenty years the open land at the Waitara has with the Taranaki settlers been an object of almost passionate desire.

When they first landed at Taranaki, the neighbouring country was almost uninhabited. Ten or twelve years previously, a large body of the Waitara Natives, led by Rere, the father of William King, the so-called rebel chief,* had formed an expedition to the south; and taking advantage of their absence, their northern neighbours, the Waikatos, under Te Whero Whero (since better known as Potatou, the Maori King), made a raid upon Taranaki, attacked, defeated, and dispersed

---

* The term *rebel*, in its legal meaning, is not generally understood. It was admitted by the Attorney-General (Sir John Campbell), in Frost's case, "that wherever there is a *private* revenge only to be gratified, a *private* grievance to be redressed, or a *private* object to be obtained, although force may be used, and although there may be an offence against the law, it does not amount to the crime of treason." And it was maintained by Sir Fitzroy Kelly that if Frost and his followers had conspired and combined by force of arms to go and burn down the gaol at Monmouth, for the purpose of liberating Vincent and the other three prisoners that were there; and if, in order to compass that design, they had massacred a large body of the Queen's troops, though it might have been murder, and though, at the least, the very attempt would have been a high misdemeanor—generally punishable—yet it would not have amounted to high treason; because the crime of high treason consists in the compassing of some general and universal object.

the remnant of the Natives, and having overrun the country and taken many prisoners, returned with them to the north. After the marauders had retired, a few of the original occupants of the country ventured to return and take possession of their houses; and their captive relations, most of whom were afterwards released, gradually flocked back into the district, and again settled themselves upon the land. The Waikato raid greatly complicated the question of Native title, and the difficulty of providing for the unfortunate immigrants, sent out by the Company before land had been procured for them, became daily more apparent. The Chief of the Waikatos claimed a certain right over the country by right of conquest; and so far as he took actual possession, his claim, according to Native usage, would be valid. It appeared, however, that he did not permanently occupy the soil; but being a Chief of great influence, with might, if not right, on his side, it was deemed expedient by the Government to buy up his interest and satisfy his claim.

The members of the Waitara tribe who happened to be in the south at the time of the Waikato invasion, maintained that they had not forfeited their right to the land by their temporary absence. "The Europeans were wrong," said William King, and other Ngatiawa Chiefs, addressing Governor Fitzroy, in the year 1844, "in striving for this land, which was never sold by its owners, the men of Ngatiawa. Now when the Ngatiawa Tribe went to Kapiti, they left some men behind on our lands, who were surprised by the Waikatos, and led away captive, who, having arrived at Waikato, were afterwards returned to Waitara to dwell there. Others came back from Kapiti. We love the land of our ancestors. We did not receive any of the goods of Colonel Wakefield (the New Zealand Company's Agent). It was wrong to buy the land which belonged to other men. There are many Chiefs to whom the land belongs who are now at Waikanae and Arapoa. It was love for the lands of our forefathers that brought us back to those lands. Friend Governor, our thoughts are that the lands were never settled by the Waikatos."* And the claims of those members of the tribe, who were

* According to Maori usage, the conquering tribe never claimed the land of the conquered, unless they took *immediate possession*, by exercising acts of ownership, such as living upon and cultivating the soil.

absent in the south when the Waikatos overran the country, and of those who had been carried away captive, and of the remnant who were left in the district (if they had ever been forfeited), according to the evidence given by the Native Secretary before the House of Representatives, were afterwards *readmitted* by the Government; and the Tribe has since been recognized and dealt with as the owners of the soil. But amongst the Tribe itself, who appear to have had almost a passionate attachment to the district, the Waitara had many claimants, and it was not without difficulty that they could for a length of time be prevailed upon to alienate any part of it; and seeing the many disadvantages of the site fixed upon by the Company for their settlement, and seeing no peaceable solution of the difficulties by which the settlers were surrounded, the expediency of breaking up the settlement was seriously entertained by the authorities more than fifteen years before the commencement of the recent outbreak.

As land for the purposes of the settlement had only been obtained in detached blocks, the settlers and the Natives were settled together in closer proximity at Taranaki than in any other of the

New Zealand settlements. Relieved from all fear of a second Waikato raid, and following the example of their English neighbours, the Natives of Taranaki soon became extensive cultivators of the soil, and the proprietors of a large amount of valuable farming stock and agricultural implements. Comparing the condition of the resident Natives with that of their countrymen in the north, the Bishop of New Zealand remarked that "the coasting craft and canoes of Auckland may here be represented by the almost innumerable carts which may be seen on market days coming from north and south into the settlement." William King and his people, then occupying the Waitara, alone possessed one hundred and fifty horses, three hundred head of cattle, forty carts, thirty-five ploughs, three winnowing machines, and twenty pairs of harrows; and in the year 1855 they exported agricultural produce to the amount of upwards of 8,000*l.*; but in the midst of the general prosperity the peace of the district was disturbed by Native feuds, and the district was soon studded over with numerous Native pahs.

The earliest and most serious of these disturbances arose out of an attempt somewhat similar to that which led to the recent conflict—an attempt to purchase land without the consent of all who claimed a voice in the disposal of it. Being exposed to a continual pressure from the settlers to acquire land from the Natives, the Taranaki Land Commissioner was always in danger of being urged into undue haste in conducting his negotiations. A piece of land was offered for sale to the then Local Commissioner (Cooper) by a Native Assessor named Rawiri; but Katatore, a man of the same Tribe, and a near relation, had always expressed his intention to retain it, and threatened to oppose any one who should offer it for sale. To test Rawiri's power to dispose of the land, the Commissioner desired him to cut the boundary line; and while he and his party were engaged in the work, Katatore and his followers cautioned them to desist; firing twice into the ground by way of warning to deter them. But they still persisted, until Katatore and his people aiming a deadly volley at them, shot Rawiri and six of his followers, and wounded several others. For a length of time afterwards the relations and followers of the contending parties were engaged in a deadly fued; and two years afterwards Katatore himself was killed. Other causes of quarrel also arose amongst them; and for a period of two or three years their progress in industrial pursuits was brought entirely to a stand.

Up to this time the settlement had never been occupied as a military post; and it is singular that, throughout those Native disturbances, the settlers suffered little direct or immediate injury; but being closely intermixed with the resident Natives, who were all well armed, who occupied numerous defensible positions, and who were not unfrequently engaged in deadly strife, the settlers naturally felt their situation to be painfully insecure; and they made repeated and urgent appeals to the Colonial Government to garrison the settlement with troops. But it was believed by the authorities that the presence of a military force would excite a feeling of jealousy and irritation in the mind of the Natives, and would tend to increase rather than to obviate the danger: and that so long as they exercised ordinary caution and forbearance, the settlers would remain uninjured: while the presence of the small force then at the disposal of the Government would be insufficient to overawe and preserve peace amongst the Natives, and be calculated to give a false confidence to the settlers, and lead them to be less careful to maintain peaceful relations with their Maori neighbours: and that military operations once commenced would end in the total destruction of the settlement. This opinion was confirmed by the Native Secretary, who, being a military man, was commissioned to make a careful examination of the ground. "The country about New Plymouth," reported Major Nugent, "is very favourable for the desultory warfare of the Natives. With the exception of a narrow strip of land from one to five miles in breadth, extending along the coast, the country is a dense forest, intersected with numerous ravines: and, except on this strip of land, the country is most unsuited for the operation of English troops against a hostile Native force. The settlement extends along the coast for twenty miles; some of the settlers have penetrated eight miles into the forest; and a much larger force than Great Britain could spare for the whole Colony of New Zealand would be insufficient for the protection of the settlement: and in case of a collision between the troops and the Natives, the settlement would dwindle into a mere military post." The Executive Council of the Colony being at that time (1855) responsible to the Crown alone, advised that, looking to the unfavourable nature of that part of the country for military operations, every effort should be made to avoid the risk of hostilities with the Natives in the Taranaki district: and that as the then recent disturbances had their origin in the attempt to purchase land from the Natives with a disputed title, the Land Purchase Department should use great caution in entering into any negotiations for the purchase of land until the views of the various claimants should have been ascertained. Governor Browne soon afterwards arriving in the Colony, and having before him so significant an illustration of the danger of attempting to purchase land with a doubtful or disputed title, condemned the conduct of the Local Commissioner in commencing a survey before he was assured that all who had even a disputed claim to the land desired it should be sold: and he declined to make a demand for reparation, on the ground that "it could only be enforced at the expense of a general war, including sooner or later all the Tribes in the Northern Island.

After the settlers had long been kept in a state of ruinous uncertainty, the Local Government succeeded in completing the purchase of detached blocks of land of considerable extent for their occupation. In one instance, thirty thousand acres were obtained at the rate of tenpence per acre. But the land being for the most part heavily timbered, the open country at the Waitara continued to be regarded by the Taranaki settlers as essential to the extension of the settlement. This favoured spot, however, was highly valued by its original Native occupants, many of whom were at that time still absent in the South. "This also is the determination of our people," wrote William King to Governor Fitzroy. "Waitara shall not be given up, the men to whom it belongs will hold it for themselves; the Ngatiawa are constantly returning to their land, on account of their attachment to the land of our birth—the land which we have cultivated, and which our ancestors marked out by boundaries and delivered to us. Friend Governor! do not you love your land, England, the land of your fathers, as we also love our land at Waitara?

Friend, let your thought be good towards us. We desire not to strive with the Europeans; but at the same time we do not wish to have our land settled by them: let them be returned to the places which have been paid for by them, lest a root of quarrel remain between us and the Europeans." "There are thousands of others," says Mr. Clarke, referring to the Waikato raid, "who were not enslaved by their enemies, and who joined Rauparaha (in the South) and those of their tribe who had followed him. These parties have already returned to the possessions of their families, who claim the country by right of descent. Every acre of land there has been allotted by their ancestors to the heads of the different families, and subdivided into allotments for the different individuals: they are all marked out by natural or artificial boundaries, and each family knows what belongs to itself, and what to others. These Natives are returning to the place of their birth every day, and never will give up possession to the Europeans. One false step now must plunge us, sooner or later, into ruin—perhaps bloodshed: the Natives never will give up tamely what they consider to be their just rights." "If the Government," he added, "*are determined to put the settlers into possession of land which we cannot convince the Natives or ourselves, honestly, that they have alienated, they must do it at the point of the bayonet."*

It was not until further disturbance had occurred amongst the Natives of the District, that the Acting Governor (Wynyard) reluctantly gave way to the importunities of the settlers, and occupied Taranaki with a military force; but, as appears to have been anticipated, the arrival of the troops in 1855, intended simply as a protection to the settlers, was regarded with suspicion by the Natives. Soon after Governor Browne's arrival in the Colony, the Government was informed that it was strongly apprehended by the Taranaki Tribe (not the Ngatiawa or Waitara) that Governor Browne would differ in his views and measures from Governor Wynyard, and that, in all probability, ere long, his word would go forth to put the troops sent down here as a protecting force by the latter, into an aggressive motion, and that thus a war between the Europeans and the Aborigines would be commenced; and being still continually urged to part with the land, the Waitara Natives were troubled by similar apprehensions, until they were visited by the officer in command of the troops, who went amongst them for the purpose of explaining the reasons for which a military force had been stationed in the district. The Chief himself appears even to have had some fear of being seized suddenly like Te Rauparaha. "I assured him," said Major Nugent, "that nothing was further from my intention than to seize him treacherously in the night. He complained much of false statements which had been made against him in the local papers; and in proof that he had some ground for his complaints, I enclose copies of the last numbers of the *Taranaki Herald*, which do not disguise the wish of some of the writers in that paper to drive William King and his party away from the Waitara. Now, independently of the illegality of such a proceeding," adds Major Nugent, "the people of the Tribe have exported produce this year to the amount of between 8,000*l.* and 9,000*l.*, the greater part of the proceeds of which is spent in British manufactured goods; and consequently, indirectly, the Natives contribute a considerable sum to the revenue of the country. I have no hesitation in saying that these people, who in their position are useful and beneficial occupiers of the soil, have been on the point of being driven to become our declared enemies, and compelled to take a position in the forest, where all the discontented and troublesome characters would have assembled, and from which it would have required considerable force, and a large expenditure of money, to drive them. In the meantime the authorities would have been harassed by constant alarms, and New Plymouth might have been thrown back a generation. I think that for the present the Natives are reassured; but I cannot answer for the continuance of tranquillity between the races, so long as such inflammatory articles are published in the newspapers, in which people of much local influence do not disguise their wishes to seize upon the land of the Natives." These suspicions, however, still continued, and Governor Browne, soon after his arrival in the Colony, reported that " various portions of land have been acquired by purchase, but there is still a deficiency: and although the greater part, and all the most respectable settlers, have abstained from expressing discontent, individuals have from time to time, by letters in the newspapers, and otherwise, shown a strong desire to expel the

Natives, and take possession of the lands to which they consider themselves entitled in right of the New Zealand Company's original purchase. Such antecedents are not likely to have laid the foundation of mutual confidence, and accordingly distrust, which in most other provinces has given place to better feelings, has not done so at New Plymouth; and the old suspicion," he added, "had been revived amongst the Natives, that the Europeans would not rest until they had slain and taken possession of that which the Maories liken to Naboth's vineyard."

CHAPTER IV.

The Government urged to adopt a New System in the Purchase of Native Land.—Declaration of the Governor on the Subject. —Negotiations for the Purchase of the Waitara.—Opposition to the Sale.—Difficulty of Completing a Satisfactory Purchase. —A Survey of the Land Attempted.—Martial Law Proclaimed.—The Waitara occupied by a Military Force.

As it was found to be impossible to obtain the assent of all who had an interest in the Waitara, it was thought that some individual members, having a special interest in particular portions of the land, might be induced to sell; and the Council of the Province presented a memorial to the General Assembly in the Session of 1858, in which they complained that the system commonly adopted by the Government of acquiring the assent of every claimant to any piece of land before a purchase is made, had been found to operate injuriously to the settlement: and they urged the expediency of setting aside the Tribal right— expressing their opinion that such of the Natives as are willing to dispose of their proportion of any common land to the Government should be permitted to do so; and that the Government should compel an equitable division of such common land amongst the respective claimants on the petition of a certain proportion of them. And they added their opinion that "no danger of a war between the Government and the Natives need be apprehended from the prosecution of a vigorous policy, inasmuch as a large proportion of the Natives themselves would cordially support it, and the remainder would, from the smallness of their number, be incapable of offering an effectual resistance." But the suggestion received no countenance at that time, either from the Government or the Assembly. On the contrary, "I will never," wrote the Governor, "permit land to be taken without the consent of those to whom it belongs; nor will I interfere to compel an equitable division of common land amongst the respective claimants. This decision is not less one of expediency than of justice, for the whole of the Maori race maintain the right of the minority to prevent the sale of land held in common, with the utmost jealousy. Wi Kingi has no sort of influence with me or the Colonial Government. We believe him to be an infamous character; but I will not permit the purchase of land over which he has any right without his consent."

Early in the following year (1859) the Governor paid a visit to the settlement; and although the settlers had not cultivated more than 13,000 of the 43,000 acres of land then in their possession, and of the territory which had already been ceded by the Natives 20,000 acres of heavily timbered land still remained in the hands of the Provincial Government open for selection, the Governor was again pressed by them to obtain additional land for the extension of the settlement. "I found them," wrote the Governor, "dissatisfied with the Government, and ill pleased with the Maories, who, although they possess large tracts of land which they cannot occupy, refuse to sell any part of it: and they complain," he added, "that they had not sufficient pasturage for their flocks, and that immigrants and capitalists are driven to seek in other provinces the accommodation which Taranaki could not under present circumstances afford." And he then made the declaration to the Natives, in which he was unfortunately understood by them to announce his intention to adopt a new policy in the purchase of Native land, viz., to treat with individual claimants, to disregard the influence of the Chiefs, and to set aside the Tribal right.

At the meeting which the Governor had with the Natives, he said he never would consent to buy land without an undisputed title; he would not permit any one to interfere in the sale of land unless he owned part of it: and, on the other hand, he would buy no man's land without his consent. A Native, described in a semi-official statement of the proceedings as "Te Teira, a Waitara Native," then stated that he was anxious to sell land belonging to him; that he heard with satisfaction the declaration of the Governor referring to individual claims, and the assurance of protection that would be afforded by his Excellency. He minutely defined the boundaries of his claim, repeated that he was anxious to sell, and that he was the owner of the land he offered for sale. He then repeatedly asked if the Governor would buy his land. Mr. McLean, on behalf of his Excellency, replied that he would. Te Teira then placed a *parawai* (bordered mat) at the Governor's feet, which his Excellency accepted. This ceremony, according to Native custom, virtually placed Teira's land at Waitara in the hands of the Governor. Paora then informed the Governor that Te Teira could not sell the land he had offered without the consent of Weteriki and himself, as they had a joint interest in a portion of it. Te Teira replied to him, and was immediately followed by William King, who, before addressing the Governor, said to his people, "I will only say a few words and then we will depart," to which they assented. He then said, "Listen, Governor, notwithstanding Teira's offer, I will not permit the sale of Waitara to the Pakeha. Waitara is in my hands; I will not give it up, ekore, ekore, ekore (i. e.), I will not, I will not, I will not. I have spoken." And, turning to his tribe, added, "Arise, let us go." Whereupon he and his followers abruptly withdrew, and it is said that some of the Natives present at the meeting cautioned Teira not to embroil the country by attempting to effect the sale.*

* The maximum price which had been given for land at Taranaki was three shillings an acre; but it is believed that the District Land Purchase Commissioner was authorized to give Te Teira a *bonus* not exceeding 250*l.* for the cession of a tract of land in so advantageous a position.

Usually negotiations for the purchase of land in New Zealand are entrusted to the officers of the Land Purchase Department, but on the present occasion the Governor himself initiated the proceedings. To any one unacquainted with the Natives, the abrupt withdrawal of William King would doubtless appear offensive, and it was in fact construed by the Governor into an act of intentional disrespect; but it was simply a Native mode of signifying the emphatic determination of the Chief of his tribe to give his uncompromising opposition to the sale, and Governor Browne was no doubt afterwards considerably embarrassed by having appeared before them in the character of a land buyer, and by having given even a conditional understanding to become the purchaser of the land.

It soon appeared that the Native by whom the land was offered for sale had great difficulty in making a satisfactory title. William King, the Chief of the Waitara, acting as the representative of the Tribe, and as the guardian of the common property, resolutely opposed the sale; and numerous members of the Tribe, including several who were residing in the south and claiming to have an interest in specific portions of the block, also refused to dispose of their respective shares; and, setting aside any question of tribal right, denied the right of Te Teira to deal with any of the land comprised within the boundaries of the block, except the specific portion of it to which he was himself individually entitled. But it appears to have been determined from the outset, that this interference of the Chief of the Waitara was a mere assumption, which should be set aside, in case of need, by force. "I have little fear," said Governor Browne, officially reporting the result of his visit to Taranaki, "that William King will continue to maintain his assumed right, and I have made every preparation to enforce obedience, should he presume to do so." The Chief of the Waitara, however, did venture to maintain his right; and in the course of the following month, acting as the mouthpiece of the community, and as the guardian of the rights of those who, besides Te Teira, claimed various portions of land within the block, and who had not consented to the sale, the Chief of the Waitara addressed a written remonstrance to the Governor, claiming to be heard in their behalf. "Your letter," he says, "reached me about Te Teira and Te Ritemana's thoughts: I will not agree to our bedroom being sold (I mean Waitara here), for this bed belongs to the whole of us. You may insist, but I will never agree to it. All I have to say to you, O Governor, is, that none of this land will be given to you; never—never, not till I die. I have heard it said that I am to be imprisoned because of this land. I am very sad because of this word. Why is it? You should remember that the Maories and Pakehas are living quietly upon their pieces of land, and therefore do not you disturb them." In his letters also addressed to the Archdeacon of Kapiti some months afterwards, King uses much the same language. "I am not willing" he wrote, "that this land should be disposed of; you must bear in mind the word of Rere (his father), which he spoke to you and Mr. Williams. You know that word about Waitara.* I will not dispose of it to the Governor and Mr. McLean. Let your word to the Governor and Mr. McLean be strong, that they may cease their importunity for Waitara

* Referring to the injunction of his father, in 1840, not to sell the Waitara.

here, that we and the Pakeha may live in peace. I will not give up the land. The Governor may strike me, and without cause, and I shall die! In that case there will be no help for it, because it is an old saying, 'The man first, and then the land.' They say that Teira's piece of land belongs to him alone. No; that piece of land belongs to us all; it belongs to the orphan, it belongs to the widow. If the Governor should come to where you are, do you say a word to him."

From the moment when he offered the land for sale, Te Teira's power to dispose of it was steadily contested. The duty of inquiring into the validity of his title was entrusted to the District Land Purchaser (Mr. Parris), Mr. McLean, the head of the Land Purchase Department, being engaged at the time in a distant part of the Colony. After a lapse of some time spent in the inquiry, Mr. Parris reported that, in the face of opposing claims, the purchase could not yet be safely completed, and some months again elapsed without his being able to make any satisfactory report of his proceedings; but he was informed, by the then Native Minister, that the Governor felt that it was impossible for him, as her Majesty's representative, to withdraw from the position he had deliberately assumed; and the Governor now directed that the purchase should, if possible, be closed without delay. "Instructions should be sent to Taranaki," he wrote in a memorandum of the 27th of August, "to close the purchase of Teira's land, which was commenced when I was there, without delay if possible. There is little chance of Mr. McLean reaching Taranaki for some time." "The Governor," wrote also the Native Minister to Mr. Parris at the same time, "is very anxious about the completion of the purchase from Teira. I am sure you will press the matter as fast as appears prudent. It will satisfy his Excellency if, without writing officially, you will let me hear privately how things stand. I have been in hopes that Mr. McLean's visit would effect something—but he delays so long." "The Governor," he added, "feels pledged to effect the purchase." The local Land Purchaser, however, who appears to have exercised great prudence and caution, and to have fairly set before the Government the difficulties that stood in the way of a peaceable purchase of the land, was still unable to hold out any hope of a speedy and satisfactory settlement of the question. "I have been investigating Teira's question," he informed the Native Minister (Sept. 21st), "in order to give an opinion as to the opposition likely to be offered to it, and I am sorry to say that I find William King full of his dogged obstinacy, assuming the right to dictate authority over land offered by the rightful owners to the Government. He takes this ground, not being able to refute the claims of Teira and his supporters, who, from all I can gather from disinterested Natives, are the rightful owners. Teira is emboldened by the justice of his claims. I therefore find it necessary to restrain him in many of his propositions, lest anger should arise and violence ensue. He offers to cut the line, but at present I decline to give my assent, knowing the opposition he is sure to meet with. The prevailing opinion amongst the Natives is that Teira's offer will settle the question of the sale of land for a long time; if purchased, more will immediately follow; if not purchased, those who want to sell will be afraid to move in the matter." And a few days afterwards the local Land Purchaser received authority from the Governor to make an immediate advance in part payment for the land. "Should you be able," wrote the Assistant Native Secretary, "to satisfy yourself that the parties offering it have an indisputable title, you will, however, inform Te Teira that the purchase will not be completed until Mr. McLean visits Taranaki." The inquiry, however, was still prolonged; "but not," it was said, "from any doubt that existed as to the title, but in the hope that the opposing party might be brought to reason." Two months afterwards, however, an instalment was paid. "I do not wish," said the Chief of the Waitara, who still persisted in his opposition, "that the land should be disturbed; and though they" (Teira and others) "have floated it, I will not let it go to sea. It is enough, Parris; their bellies are full with the sight of the money you have promised them; but don't give it to them; if you do, I won't let you have the land, but will take it and cultivate it myself." "Teira stops in town," added Mr. Pariss, reporting the proceedings, "since he received the instalment, considering it not safe to stop at Waitara." On the same occasion a document setting forth the boundaries of the block was read to the assembled Natives by

Mr. Parris. Appended to the document was a declaration on behalf of the Governor, that if any man could prove his claim to any piece of land within the boundary described, such claim would be respected, and the claimant might hold or sell as he thought fit. But all claimants appeared to be immediately afterwards shut out by a statement authoritatively made and widely circulated amongst the Natives in all parts of the country, that the purchase-money having been paid to Teira, the whole of the land had become the property of the Crown. Still the opposition continued, and there appeared to be no prospect of obtaining undisputed title to the land; but feeling himself committed to effect the purchase, the Governor consulted the Executive Council on the subject (January 25th, 1860), who advised that, should William King or any other Native endeavour to prevent the survey, or in any way interfere with the prosecution of the work—that the surveyor's party should be protected, during the whole performance of the work, by military force; that the Commanding Officer should be empowered to subject the Province to martial law, and that he should be instructed to keep possession of the debateable land, if necessary, by force of arms. But before attempting a survey of the land, Mr. Parris, the District Commissioner, made a last ineffectual effort to obtain William King's concurrence in the sale. "I was with him and his people," he reported, "on Monday last, and went fully into the question with them, informing them of the determination of the Government in the matter. I endeavoured to work upon them by explaining to them how very much the Government had been troubled with the Waitara question; that it was their duty to endeavour to meet the Government in this matter, and settle the question without any unpleasantness. In reply," continued the Report, "a young man named Hemi Te Koro spoke favourably; but before he had finished, William King, perceiving the tendency of his views, got up and said, 'I will not consent to divide the land, because my father's dying words and instructions were to hold it.'" A few days afterwards (February 20th), the survey was commenced; but being obstructed, though without violence, the attempt was for the time abandoned. "It was the wife of Wiremu Patukakawiki and their own two daughters, and some other women of their *hapus*," said the Reverend Rewai Te Ahan, "who drew off the Governor's surveyors from their own pieces of land." In reporting the obstruction to the Secretary of State, the Governor says "that no violence was offered by the Natives"—a statement confirmed by one of the local newspapers, which reported that the obstruction was managed in the least objectionable way possible, and that no more violence was used than was necessary to prevent the extension of the chain.*

2 ~~Ten~~ days afterwards, although there was no disturbance of the public peace, martial law was proclaimed, and a manifesto was published by the authorities in the Maori language, and widely circulated by special agents amongst all the Tribes

---

* "Last Monday (February 20th), was the day; and, on laying down the chain, this was obstructed by a parcel of old Maori women, sent by William King and his people, to prevent by main force (although without arms) the surveyors from going on with the survey. Mr. Carrington, one of the surveyors, was embraced by one of the old hags, together with his theodolite, and prevented from using it, and the chain was forcibly taken away, but was recovered; a reserve of men was stationed near the old witches, in case they were not able to resist the survey; but the women were too much for our surveyors, and they were compelled ignominiously to retreat."—*Correspondent of the "Southern Cross."*

of the Northern Island, declaring that Te Teira's title had been carefully investigated and found to be good; that it was not disputed by any one; that payment for the land had been received by Te Teira; and that the land now belonged to the Queen: and shortly afterwards (March 5) the Queen's Troops were marched out to the Waitara, and themselves or their Native allies destroyed the homesteads of William King and his people, took military possession of the ground, and thus dispossessed by force the occupants of the soil.

CHAPTER V.

Memorial to the Governor warning him not to proceed, and showing the Rights of the Native Occupants of the Land.—Rank and Position of the Principal Opponent of the Sale.—Apprehension amongst the Natives excited by the forcible Occupation of the Waitara.—Remonstrances of the Absentee Claimants and others.—Their Petition to the Queen for the Governor's Recal.

BEFORE military occupation was taken of the Waitara, an appeal was made to the Governor by one of the settlers, showing that William King, being the Chief of the Waitara, it was no mere assumption on his part to claim to have a voice as to the disposal of the land, more especially as many who had never been consulted had claims to specific portions of the block: urging, at the same time, that a complete public and impartial investigation * should be made, and deprecating

* "Had such a tribunal existed, there is little doubt but that the Waitara misunderstanding would have been satisfactorily adjusted. At any rate, her Majesty's representative would have occupied a more dignified position than the one he holds in the case as prosecutor, judge and jury."—*George Clarke.*

in the most earnest manner the employment of military force. "It is with the deepest surprise and sorrow," he wrote, "that your petitioner has heard that a resort to arms, in order to enforce an alleged purchase of an insignificant block of land at the Waitara, may be almost immediately expected; your petitioner advisedly uses the word 'alleged,' as he cannot possibly believe that your Excellency's Government would consider such purchase as a *de jure* or even a *de facto* one; much less, that they would attempt to take forcible possession of the block referred to, were they thoroughly cognizant of the real facts and circumstances. Your petitioner fully believes that a thorough and impartial investigation, with due publicity, at a full meeting of all the Waitara Natives on the spot, would elicit the following facts, viz.: in portions of that block, several Natives, whose claims are presumably unknown to the District Land Commissioner, have also, like Teira, a *bonâ fide* individual or private interest; while, over the whole block, rides the Tribal or public interest. William King admits that he himself has no individual or private interest in this particular block; but (which is perfectly consistent with such admission) he rightfully claims, as the principal Chief of the Waitara Tribe, and as the acknowledged representative of the great majority of the same Tribe, that the individual or private interests referred to, and also such over-riding Tribal or public interest, should be alike respected and held inviolate by the Government. Were the whole Tribe at the Waitara consenting, the title would of course be clear enough, and the purchase a good, complete, and amicable one; but Teira, so far from having the whole tribe, has only an inconsiderable fraction in his favour; while against him is arrayed the great majority, with the principal Chief at their head. Did that majority consent, William King would also consent as a matter of course, he being, in that respect, the mouth-piece (as it were) of the great majority; but until such majority do actually consent, William King's concurrence could not justly bind them, and also could not possibly be of any avail, except as a mere pretext for an unjust war like the one which is said to be in agitation." The preceding statements contain a correct summary of the Maori unwritten law or custom of real property throughout the Island, and at the Waitara in particular. "However inconvenient such real property law may be to the Colonists, or detrimental to the Aborigines themselves, it cannot be forcibly abolished without glaring injustice, and the almost certain risk of an internecine war between the two races throughout the Colony. That war, at all times a calamity, would, under such circumstances, be also a crime. That as to the block before referred to, it appears in the highest degree objectionable that the District Land Commissioner should, directly or indirectly, decide on the title of owners—tribal or individual, absent or present, dissenting or consenting—in short, should, virtually, decide on the validity of his own alleged purchase, and finally, in order to enforce his own *ex parte* decision, should, in effect, have and exercise the dread power of declaring war: thus resting in one subordinate officer ministerial, judicial, and dictatorial functions. Further, it would seem that Teira's allegation of his own absolute interest— the allegation of one who has received British gold, and who believes that he will be backed by British bayonets—the allegation of one who shows himself ready, for the sake of lucre, to destroy his own tribe and his own race, and to plunge the whole Colony into unspeakable calamity—is to be accepted as final and conclusive, so as to weigh down the unanimous testimony of the great majority of the Tribe, who, unseduced by money, and unintimidated by power, are prepared to seal their testimony with their own life-blood. Here at present there is (from various reasons, too numerous to mention) a dead silence; no voice is raised at this, the eleventh hour. Your petitioner has, therefore, attempted a feeble cry; but do not, let me beseech your Excellency, despise the cause, on account of the feebleness, the informality, or the temerity of its advocates, for the cause is a good and noble one: it is not the cause of this or that individual, of this or that section of Colonial society, but of humanity and of justice." It was not until nearly a year after the war commenced that it was publicly known that such an appeal had been addressed to the Governor before the Troops were marched into the field. The appeal, however, was made in vain. Before it reached the Governor, martial law had been proclaimed, and it was probably thought that it was now too late to recede, without compromising the dignity of the representative of the Crown: and the Queen's Troops were marched upon the ground.

The most satisfactory evidence of the valid purchase of land from the Natives, is the fact that a survey has been made of it, and that the boundaries have been marked out upon the ground without opposition, and without calling forth any adverse or unsatisfied claim. In case the survey is interrupted or opposed, the usual course is, not to proceed with the work until the validity of the claims has been inquired into; but in the case of the Waitara purchase, it appears to have been predetermined that the survey should be carried out regardless of any opposition that might be offered, and that the land should be occupied by military force.

A few days after the Troops had taken possession, a small party of about seventy Natives, who had been driven from the land, returned; and, for the purpose of asserting their title, and of keeping alive their claim, built a stockade within the limits of the debateable land. It was afterwards admitted by the local authorities " that no one had decided that the Pah was not built on ground belonging to persons who built it;" but the Officer in command of the Troops immediately (March 17th) took up a position before it, and sent a summons to its occupants to surrender, which, however, they would neither read nor receive. "The guns and rockets," he reported, "now opened fire upon the Pah at about seven hundred yards, and in half an hour I moved to the right, to batter another face at shorter range, when the Natives opened fire upon us." Thus hostilities commenced, the first shot being fired by the Troops. A heavy fire was afterwards kept up against the stockade with shot and shell, one hundred and thirty rounds being fired from the howitzers, besides the rockets. In justification of these proceedings, it has been said that "to hesitate about abstract right is to perpetuate disorder;" and it was also affirmed that "the Governor being of right the sole judge of questions respecting Native territorial claims, was justified in enforcing his jurisdiction in the only practical mode, viz., by military occupation." Yet, assuming that the stockade was built on ground belonging to those who built it, it is difficult to see what justification can be pleaded for this deadly attack upon the Queen's subjects.

If active military operations had been undertaken in the name of the Crown, for the purpose of bringing a murderer to justice, or of repressing some serious disturbance of the public peace, or of carrying out the judgment of some legal tribunal, these proceedings would have excited no jealous apprehension in the Native mind. Nearly twenty years before, when the Natives were much more numerous than they now are, and when there was not a single company of soldiers stationed in the colony, a young Native Chief of consequence, belonging to an influential Tribe, was tried with all the solemn form and ceremony of English law, and convicted of the wilful murder of an English family, and publicly executed in the most densely peopled district in New Zealand, without the slightest disturbance of the public peace, and the justice and daring of the act inspired the Natives with respect and confidence. But when the Queen's Troops were marched to the Waitara, and when William King and his people, who for years had occupied the ground, were forcibly driven off, and the Troops were seen to take possession of land, the title to which was disputed, and which for years the Native owners had in vain been importuned to sell, it is hardly surprising that they were irritated to see their old suspicion restored, that "the Europeans would not rest until they had slain and taken possession;" that they should regard the intentions of the Government with suspicion and distrust; and that, fearing a common danger, Natives in other parts of the country should take up arms in support of William King.

The conduct of the Chief of the Waitara, in opposing the sale, had always been consistent, and his language appeared to be that of a Chief engaged in maintaining what he believed to be a rightful claim; but it was represented, by those who were anxious to acquire the land, as that of a man interposing an illegitimate authority, to prevent the true owners of the land from ceding it to the Crown; and an attempt was made to depreciate his rank and position in the Tribe. But the Native Secretary, reporting an interview with him as long ago as 1855, speaks of him naturally, and of course, as the "principal Chief of the Waitara." "On our arrival," wrote Major Nugent, "the whole Tribe assembled, and after one of the Chiefs had briefly stated the reports that they had heard, William King, the principal Chief of Waitara, arose and spoke for some time; and the Chiefs of a neighbouring tribe speaking of him about the same time, said, 'William King being *the head Chief* of all Waitara on both sides of it, it was for himself to choose and say on which side of it he was to reside.'" And the attempt which was afterwards made, to raise Te Teira to equal rank with William King, was treated by the Natives with derision. "You say," referring to Teira, said a Chief of Hawkes Bay, "because his genealogy was published last winter, therefore he is a Chief. What, indeed, about his genealogy? William King would never give his genealogy, because it is known throughout this island; it is not recounted. This is a thing for the common man to do, who never was heard of before. I know that man Teira, that he is a man of little note; Wiremu Kingi is their great man, heard of and known by all the Tribes; but Teira's name is Manuka—even Tea-tree—*Scrub,* and nothing more." No one, in fact, can read the voluminous official documents on the subject of Taranaki without seeing that

William King was always regarded by successive Governors, and by all the civil servants, as the *de facto* lord of the manor of Waitara. But as he was looked upon as the principal obstacle to the acquisition of the land, he had always been unpopular with the Taranaki settlers.

There is no doubt, however, that while he was residing in the South, he was considered to have done good service to the Government, and to have proved himself to be a staunch ally. After the fatal catastrophe at the Wairau, when the settlement of Wellington (then utterly defenceless) was threatened by Te Rauparaha, William King, then residing at Waikanae, had nearly 1,000 well-armed men who obeyed his orders, and to his loyalty alone was attributed the failure of Te Rauparaha's schemes; and more recently, during the disturbances near Wellington in 1846-7, he joined his forces with our Troops, and was declared by authority to have been mainly instrumental in driving Rangihaeta from the bush. But notwithstanding his public services, he received no welcome from the Taranaki settlers; and as his return to the Waitara in 1848 diminished their hope of obtaining possession of that district, his arrival was regarded by them almost in the light of a public calamity.*

Though the Waitara Natives had many sympathizers in all parts of the country, the number of Natives belonging to other Tribes who actually went to Taranaki to join them, was by no means considerable; but the feeling of dissatisfaction and distrust excited in their minds by the conduct of the authorities in taking possession of Native land by force, was almost universal. "Everything," as Sir William Martin observed, "tended to strengthen the notion, already generally entertained amongst the Natives, that the Government cared for nothing so much as to get land. Can we be surprised that the old feeling of distrust acquired at once a new strength, and spread rapidly through the widely scattered settlements of the Ngatiawa Tribe? Nor could it be confined even to that Tribe. The sense of a common interest, a common peril, carried it onward through the country; and

* "During the two years that I knew William King at Waikanae, I always found him exceedingly quiet and well-disposed. He was always most attentive to his religious duties; and during school-hours he was constantly to be found in his place with the rest of his people, thus encouraging them by his example, and was undoubtedly a warm support to the *Rev. Samuel Williams.*

when at last force was resorted to, the feeling of alarm and irritation reached its height. These men, the Maories, chafe under the sense of what they believe to be a great wrong. They are bitterly disappointed. They ask why a Government, which had been constantly urging them to settle their own disputes by peaceable means, should itself resort at once to armed force? Why such force is employed, not to punish crime, but to seize land? They ask why is William King, our old ally, now treated as an enemy? Why does the Pakeha denounce without measure the slaughter of the five men at Omata, committed after hostilities had commenced, while Ihaia, the contriver of a most foul and treacherous murder, is received by us as a friend and ally? Such men unwillingly accept the answers which are too readily suggested: William King will not part with the Waitara; Ihaia is willing to sell land."

As regards the Waitara, too, it has always been especially valued by the Native owners. "From ancient Maori traditions," says the late Protector of Aborigines, "it appears that this land had been in possession of the tribe from time immemorial;

that it is dear to them from the fact that it is the spot on which their forefathers landed when they emigrated to this country; that on this account the place is sacred ground to them, so much so that when the New Zealand Company's purchase was made at Taranaki, Wiremu Kingi's father, as head of his Tribe, and again, some time after, with his dying breath, solemnly charged his son never to give up the possession of their ancestors to the Pakeha." "Brothers," said a Red Indian Chief in a Council held by the Cherokees, " brothers, we have heard the words of the great father: he is very good; he says that he loves his red children. Brothers, when the first white man came among us, the Muscozins gave him ground and lighted a fire to warm him. When the pale faces of the South waged war against him, our young warriors drew their tomahawks and shielded his head from the scalping-knife. But when the white man was warmed by the fire lighted by Indians, and had fattened on Indian liberality, he became very great; the summits of mountains did not stop him, and his feet covered plains and valleys, his arms extended to the two seas. Then he became our great father. He loved his red children; but he said, 'You had better move a little farther, lest I unintentionally tread on you,' and with one foot he pushed red men beyond the sea, and with the other he trampled on the graves of their ancestors. But our great father loves his red children, and soon held to them another language. He spoke a great deal, but what he said meant nothing but 'Move farther off, you are still too near me.' I have heard many speeches of our great father, but all begin and end in the same way. Brothers, when he spoke to us on a preceding occasion, he said to us, 'Go a little farther, you are still too near: go beyond the Oconce, and the Oakmulyo, there is an excellent country;' he also added, 'This land is yours for ever after.' And now he says, 'The country in which you are settled belongs to you, but go to the other side of the Mississippi, where there is plenty of game; there you may remain as long as the grass grows and the water flows.' Brothers, will not our great father join us there also, for he loves his red children, and has a forked tongue." When Captain Hobson was seeking to induce the Natives of New Zealand to sign the treaty of Waitangi, by engaging, in the name of her Majesty, that it should be for their own advantage to become the subjects of the Crown, he, too, was believed by many of them, to whom the fate of the Aborigines of other countries appeared to have been known, to be speaking with a forked tongue. "Send the man away," said one of them;. "do not sign the paper; if you do you will be reduced to the condition of slaves, and be obliged to break stones for the roads. Your land will be taken from you, and your dignity as Chiefs will be destroyed." They had heard, they said, the history of our conduct to the Aborigines of America and Australia, and could not but be jealous of our object in seeking to gain a footing in the country. Great pains have indeed been taken by successive Governors, missionaries, and ministers of religion, and by all persons in authority, to satisfy them of our disinterested intentions: but the forcible occupation by the Queen's troops of a much valued tract of Native land excited a distrustful feeling in their minds; and, alarmed at the growing greatness of the white man, and seeing that "the summits of mountains do not stop him— that his feet cover plains and valleys, and that his arms extend to the two seas"—the Maories are becoming possessed by an instinctive misgiving that they will soon be thrust aside to make way for the insidious stranger.

Grave remonstrances against the proceedings of the Government poured in from all parts of the country, expressed in all cases with great point and force, and not unfrequently in the most touching language. "The reason why I write to you is this," said one of the Natives, referring to the sale by Teira, "that I feel concerned for the Pakehas who are living in peace, and for the Maories also who are living in peace, lest they be dragged by his evil deeds and get into trouble, because I am certain they will get into trouble." " Friends, companions, brothers, farewell, and abide where you are with the people of your friends, and your fathers. Listen, Rewai, and your people, and our Father Hadfield. Here is death—I mean Waitara; the Pakeha is now taking it." "Now," wrote the Reverend Rewai Ahau to the Superintendent of Wellington, "we thought that the intentions of the Governor would not be different from those of the other Governors who preceded him. Now, we are perplexed and say, 'Well, these are new regulations from our Queen; but we suppose that the Governor has, perhaps, been deceived by Teira and his companions, and by his Land Purchaser at Taranaki; and therefore he has so lately sent his soldiers to Waitara to frighten all the men and the women who drove off his surveyors from the land which was their property and ours, and to take it without paying us.' * * * I say, in conclusion, that I cannot find words to pacify my Tribe, that they may be no longer irritated about our land; they are very sore that the land of our ancestors should be taken without their consent. If that land should be permanently taken, it will be a permanent saying, down to future generations, that the land was violently taken by the Queen of England's Governor. And where is the help now," he concludes, "with which the Governor requites Wiremu Kingi? Wiremu Kingi always was one who upheld the Government. He never in any way recognized the Maori King up to the time of the fighting about Waitara."

Six months after the commencement of hostilities, several of the Waitara Natives, who were then residing in the south, formally addressed the Superintendent of Wellington on the subject. "We have portions of land," they say, "at Waitara, within the piece of land which was wrongly sold by Teira to the Governor, as well as those who were driven off that piece of land. It belongs to our ancestors. We ask this question. What are we peaceable persons, who are not joining in the fighting, to do when our lands are wrongfully taken by the Governor? Where shall we seek a way by which we may get our lands restored to us? Shall we seek it from the Queen, or from whom? We imagined that it was for the law to rectify wrongs. Up to this time, our hearts keep anxiously inquiring. We will say no more. From us members of Ngatiawa, and owners of that land at Waitara." "Birds," said William Thompson, " do not cry unless there be an enemy in sight, except indeed in the morning and evening. At daybreak their song is heard; and at the twilight again, but not in the daytime unless some bird of prey appears. They sit quietly in the branches of the trees and make no noise, until they see the great bird, the hawk, that comes to destroy them; then all cry out, great birds and small. There is a general cry." (Meaning, we were quiet and should have remained so, had not a great bird disturbed us and aroused our fears.)

"Who caused the pain?" said Renata, the

eloquent spokesman of the Ngatikahuhuna Tribe. "I take it to have been the Governor. Very different were the land-purchasing arrangements of former days. There was to be an assemblage; and when they had all consented, then the land should pass. All the Maories heard this from the Governor. But now they hear—eh? this plan of buying is changed, and land is now to be sold by a single individual. Sir, this is the way by which this pain, this trouble, has come upon us; it was through double-dealing that this trouble came. Had the old way continued, we should not have gone wrong; but since it has been abandoned, and attention has been paid to a single individual, difficulties have arisen. Sir, all these evils are of your doing. First, there was the wish to take our lands, and now is the accomplishment of it; for the cause (of the war) was but a small matter, and you have gone on importing Pakehas from other lands to fight with the Maories. The next thing will be, you will hide your error under the cloak of the Waikatos having gone to Taranaki to ward off the weapon raised by you against William King, whereas your opposition was made in order that you might get the land. But you say that man,

William King, must let down his bristles, and pay obeisance to his Sovereign the Queen. This is the answer: Sir, what then is the Maori doing? The Maori is yielding obedience; for many years he has been listening to that teaching of the Queen's. But the Governor has made it all go wrong. Your word is not clear. Perhaps you think he is not a man, that you say he should not raise his bristles when his land is taken from him? If your land were taken by a Maori, would your bristles not rise? Give him back his land, and then if we see his bristles still sticking up, I will admit that you are right. You quote from the Scripture that children should obey their parents; quote to the Governor the other portion of the same passage, 'Fathers, provoke not your children to wrath.'"

On all former occasions of dissatisfaction, the Natives had been instructed that instead of taking up arms, and resorting to force for the redress of their grievances, they ought to appeal to the law, or seek for protection by petition to the Queen,* who, though far away, they were taught to believe is ever mindful of their interests; and several hundred of the Natives residing in the South

* See Note, *ante*, Chapter II. p. 46.

addressed a memorial to Her Majesty, praying for the Governor's recal. "This," said the memorialists, "is the memorial (*lit.* lamentation) of us your loving children, (sighing) under the darkness which has at this present time befallen us. The Governor has unwarrantably proceeded to take possession of land of a certain Chief at Taranaki, named Wiremu King. The Governor purchased it from a Native named Te Teira; he has fought about that land, and fired upon the people of that place. They were loving subjects of yours. Their object was not to trample upon the law, but rather to retain possession of the land handed down to them by their ancestors and by their father. They did not wish to sell that land. This unwarrantable proceeding of this Governor has occasioned grief and confusion to all of us, because we know that this system is not yours; thus taking away, without cause, the land of every person, and of the orphan and widow." An attempt was made to discredit this memorial; and in this instance those who signed it received, in the name of her Majesty, a curt and discouraging reply. But there is no doubt that it expressed the feeling of thousands; and that the loyalty of her Majesty's Maori subjects was most severely tried, "My heart," said one of our most staunch allies, "is split asunder; half of it is with the Pakeha who was my teacher, the other is with the Maories who are my brothers,"—a sentiment which throughout New Zealand then painfully divided the hearts of the most loyal of her Majesty's Native subjects. And but for their knowledge of the fact that they had "sturdy friends," who, both in the Assembly and elsewhere, at the risk of being charged with having forgotten their allegiance, manfully espoused their cause; and but for the belief that the Natives entertained that the Queen of England would yet redress the wrong, and condemn the policy of the then Colonial rulers, there is reason to believe that they would have been driven to make common cause, and to join in a general resistance to what they believed to be the injustice of our rule.

CHAPTER VI.

Question of Title.—Disastrous Consequences to the Taranaki Settlement, from the forcible Occupation of the Waitara.—Popularity of the Government Policy.—Debates in the General Assembly.—Sir William Martin's Pamphlet on the " Taranaki Question."—" Notes by the Governor."

" THE question of title," it has been said, " is one on which persons not versed in the intricacies of Native usage cannot expect to form an independent judgment; and, in the management of Native affairs, the Governor of New Zealand commonly acts with the assistance of the Officers of the Native Department, who from their knowledge of the language, character, and customs, of the Natives, are supposed to be qualified to give him accurate information and reliable advice." But, from the published records of the Office, it does not appear that the Native Department was consulted either as to the validity of the purchase, or as to the expediency of driving William King and his people from the Waitara, and of taking possession of the land by military force. Experience, however, has long since proved that no menaces of military interference were likely to have any effect upon men who from their childhood have been accustomed to regard it as a point of honour to shed their last drop of blood for the inheritance of their Tribe; and as not six months before the commencement of hostilities the Governor had himself reported that " the immediate consequences of any attempt to acquire Maori lands without previously extinguishing the title to the satisfaction of all having an interest in them, would be an universal outbreak, in which many innocent Europeans would perish," it is impossible to avoid the conclusion that, by whomsoever he was advised, he was entirely misled as to the completeness of the inquiry into the validity of the title, and as to the probable consequences of driving from their homesteads an influential Chief and his people by military force. But before the Governor of New Zealand can form a sound and independent judgment on important Native questions, he must have time to become acquainted with Native usages, modes of expression, and habits of thought. The late

Governor was no doubt told that William King had always been the one great obstacle to the progress of the settlement; that he had not only refused to sell his own land, but had interfered to prevent the sale of the land of others; that Te Teira and those who offered the block of land at the Waitara for sale, had an absolute right to sell it; and that whatever might be the case in other parts of the country, there existed no tribal right at the Waitara to prevent the claimants from disposing of it; that the interference of William King was an unwarrantable assumption which he would not venture to maintain; that no danger of an armed resistance need be apprehended; and, that by showing a bold front, the Governor would completely overawe him, and lay a solid foundation for the prosperity of the settlement, and earn for himself the character of the most spirited and enlightened ruler who had ever administered the Government of New Zealand. But unfortunately the persons by whose opinions the late Governor appears to have been guided, were not in a position to give him reliable advice; and urged to find an outlet for the settlers, and counselled by his Ministers that the time had arrived when it was necessary that his authority should be supported by the bayonet, he determined to occupy the land by military force.

The certain consequences of this unusual proceeding soon became apparent, and the blindness of those who urged the Governor to resort to force was visited upon the unfortunate settlers in a manner the most painful and humiliating. Within less than a fortnight after the adoption of the "vigorous policy" recommended by the Council of the Province, and which they declared would be attended by no danger of an outbreak, the Superintendent reported "that, with the exception of about ninety persons, the whole of the settlers had abandoned their homesteads, and were concentrated in the town; that, in a small town intended for a population of 1,000, upwards of 2,500 were crowded, and that nearly 500 of them were living upon rations supplied at the public expense: and he suggested that in point of economy, and for other reasons, it would be expedient to deport women and children to the number of about 600 from the Province." Whether or not their claims were valid, it was now evident that the Natives who had been forcibly dispossessed would not submit to see them set aside by force, and since blood on both sides had been shed, the Governor became alive to the dangerous consequences of commencing a survey before he was assured that all who had even a disputed claim to the land desired it should be sold. He now reported to the Duke of Newcastle that a much larger number of Troops than had hitherto been asked for would be necessary to maintain possession of the Colony at all; that he had written to the Governors of the Australian Colonies, requesting them to send him such support as they were able; and that hitherto he had considered that 2,000 men, with a strong Company of Artillery, would have enabled him to bring such a force into the field suddenly as would extinguish the first sparks of rebellion; but that he was now compelled to say that he believed 3,000 men, a steam gun-boat, and a steamer of war, would be necessary for some time to come, to ensure the maintenance of peace. Following closely upon repeated assurances that the purchase of the land had been completed fairly—that it was not disputed by any one—that the Chief of the Waitara had never asserted any title to it —and that no real opposition was expected from him — this startling intelligence surprised the British Cabinet, and drew from Sir Cornewall Lewis, then acting as Colonial Minister, a grave and significant reply.

Many months, however, elapsed before the public generally was aware how little can be effected in New Zealand by military force; and, with the insignificant number of Troops at his disposal, the situation of the Officer in command was painfully embarrassing. The Pahs of the insurgents were invariably taken, but the occupants as certainly succeeded in making their escape; and instead of gaining credit for capturing their strongholds, Colonel Gould, after being involved in an unequal contest with a formidable enemy, in an impracticable country, was given to understand that "the Maories construe escape into victory," that they must be "made to feel our power both to protect and to avenge," and that it was expected he would find some means of striking an effective blow against them. At the same time, however, the Governor was anxious to avoid unnecessary bloodshed; and two months after the commencement of hostilities he requested that Colonel Gould "would abstain from all interference with William King, unless he should himself commence hostilities." He afterwards repeated the request, and for some time there was an almost total cessation of active operations. But, unfortunately for the Officer in command, it was not then generally known that he had been prohibited from taking the offensive and attacking William King; so his unexplained inaction naturally bore the appearance of a want of energy and enterprise; and, failing to gain any decided advantage over the insurgents, Colonel Gould was assailed on all sides with the bitterest abuse.

The danger of rousing the Natives into an armed resistance was now sufficiently apparent; for with more than 2,000 British troops in the province, with the sea close at hand for the base of our operations, and with five ships of war on the New Zealand Station, the insurgents, inferior to ourselves in arms, numbers, and equipment, soon had the whole district in their power. The settlers, who bore their accumulated misfortunes with wonderful spirit, and who for several months were crowded together in a state of helpless inactivity within the narrow limits of the town,* had the mortification to see their homesteads set on fire and their cattle driven away within less than a mile of the military post. Those who ventured beyond the limits of the lines were liable to be waylaid and shot; the road to the Waitara, not more than twelve miles distant, could only be traversed in safety with a powerful military escort; and instead of convincing the Natives of our power " to protect and avenge," our protecting power, as had been frequently foretold, was seen to be practically limited within gunshot of the camp.

It appears to have been determined that the public should have no opportunity of expressing any opinion either as to the justice or policy of occupying the land by a military force; thus the determination of the Executive to have recourse to force, in case of need, to gain possession of the land, was designedly concealed, on the ground that the public discussion of the question would have been likely to produce more harm than good;

---

* The area within the trenches, in which nearly the whole population were for a length of time cooped up, did not exceed thirty acres.

and when, to the astonishment of the community, martial law was proclaimed, few of the settlers were sufficiently informed on the subject to form any opinion of the merits of the case. It was officially stated by the authorities that the Native was in arms against the Queen's sovereign authority; that the Chief of the Waitara had never possessed or asserted any title to the land; that he was a lawless and turbulent member of a powerful and mischievous anti-land-selling league; that the title of the seller had been carefully investigated, and found to be valid; that to enforce the purchase would be to protect the weak against the strong, and would tend to the speedy acquisition of large tracts of valuable land, not only in the Province of Taranaki, but in other parts of the country. Under these circumstances, and looking to the opinion frequently expressed by the Governor, of the danger of attempting to buy land with a disputed title, it was naturally believed that the Government would not have risked a Native insurrection by enforcing the purchase of a small tract of land, the title to which was open to the slightest doubt. And, as the expenses of the war were to be borne by Great

Britain, the local Government, on opening the session, informed the General Assembly that they had received from all parts of the Colony assurances of sympathy and support. Seeing that these statements were made on the authority of the Government, it is hardly surprising that their policy was afterwards supported by a majority in both Houses of the Colonial Parliament. In the Upper House, the war party were as three to one, and the former Attorney-General of the Colony was the only member who raised his voice in opposition. In the House of Representatives, parties were more nearly balanced. The Ministers confidently maintained the validity of the purchase, but they showed no desire to have the case investigated by competent authority, and they succeeded in defeating a motion for a Committee of Inquiry. But Native interests were not without powerful advocates in the Assembly; and the case of the Natives was supported with great spirit by the Superintendent of the Province of Auckland, the Superintendent of the Province of Wellington, by the leader of the opposition, by the Chairman of Committees, and by other leading members of the Assembly.

"Whenever *land* was spoken of," said Mr. Carleton, "the suspicion of the Natives was raised. The influence of the Native Secretary's Department had been entirely destroyed by its having been connected with the Land Purchase Department; the Governor had lost his influence through having become the chief land broker. The Natives felt that the Governor was no longer a judge between themselves and the Land Purchaser." And he maintained that inquiry should be made into the circumstances of the case; and, if injustice should be found to have been done, that restitution should be made. "The land," he declared, "was the bone in this case; if wrongly acquired, we had to give it up. For the quarrel was not confined to Taranaki; we had lost the confidence of three-fourths of the Natives, who believed that the intention of the Government was to take their lands by force. If we desired to avert a war of races, we must begin by placing ourselves *recti in curiâ*. War was a heavy responsibility. It was all very well for those outside the House to rant about 'putting down the Natives,' but the case was very different within. They had votes; each Member in the House exercised one-fortieth part of the Government of the country. They knew what a fearful thing it was to have upon their conscience the reckless shedding of blood in an unjust cause."

The leader of the opposition, afterwards Colonial Prime Minister, Mr. Fox, attacked the policy of the Government without the slightest affectation of reserve. "Having," as he declared, "neglected the machinery of friendly influence and of political institutions, having taught the Natives that they were regarded as a separate and independent people," his Excellency next invited them to arm themselves for the impending struggle! In 1857, long after the King movement was in full progress —long after the signs of disaffection were manifest to every one—his Excellency, for no assignable or conceivable reason, repealed, by proclamation, those wise restrictions on the sale of arms and ammunition which his predecessor had imposed; and thus, not only invited, but enabled the Natives to do what they had since most effectually done— arm themselves to the teeth, from one end of the Island to the other! And now, having prepared them for the struggle, he took steps to bring it on. He effected this importunate, this ill-judged, this ill-timed, this incomplete purchase of that miserable 600 acres, of which we have heard so much. Why did he, at such a critical time, add this culminating cause of war to the others less threatening? Why was it necessary to buy, why necessary to survey, why necessary to take possession, at this particular crisis? I greatly fear, sir," the honourable member continued, "that other motives operated in producing the inconsiderate rashness with which this purchase was effected—unconsciously, perhaps, to his Excellency, but, nevertheless, influencing his mind. When I reflect on the fact that ever since the reversal of Mr. Spain's award the settlers at Taranaki have looked with a longing eye on the fat and fertile fields at Waitara—when I remember that the Native Minister is a representative of the Province of Taranaki and doubt not that his constituents often pressed him on the subject—when, above all, I refer to that petition of the Provincial Council of Taranaki which proposes to the Governor to compel a dissentient minority, or even majority of the Natives, to divide their common lands with a view to a sale, and which assures his Excellency that he need not fear to attempt such compulsion, 'because the dissentients would be few in number, and incapable of offering any resistance,' I cannot help fearing that his Excellency has been influenced by a pressure from without, which has forced him into a course from which the least foresight ought to have withheld him."

"While honestly and conscientiously believing," said Dr. Featherston, the Superintendent of the Province of Wellington, concluding an eloquent speech, "that the war is an unjust and unholy war, I cannot but feel that we are placed in a most painful position; for while, on the one hand, any retreat or vacillation in carrying on the war might be most disastrous to both races, it is, on the other hand, most shocking to urge that we should go on shedding blood in a cause which we believe to be unjust. I cannot but express an earnest hope that we may be able to devise some means of bringing the conflict to a close without compromising the dignity of the Crown, or the safety of both races. I would remind you that, as the Natives have not in this House any representatives of their race, we are bound by a sense of justice— by that love of fair play which ever has been, and, I trust, ever will be, the distinguishing characteristic of our nation—to protect their interests; to mete out equal justice. For my own part, I know of no higher duty that can possibly devolve upon this House than to prove to the Natives that it is a tribunal to which an appeal for redress will never be made in vain. I can conceive no means so calculated to restore the confidence of the Natives in the justice of the Government (which has been so entirely destroyed by these transactions), as a determination evinced by this House to protect them from acts of injustice, no matter how high the powers by which they are perpetrated. Such, I repeat, is the most sacred duty that can possibly devolve upon this House." And a large portion of the time of the session was afterwards devoted by the House to a patient and a painstaking endeavour to grapple with the difficulties of the Native question; and one of the oldest and most trusted friends of the Natives was able to record his opinion "that the rights of the Natives were nobly vindicated by the independent representatives of the people." *

* The Superintendent of the Province of Wellington, in his speech on opening the Council of the Province, expressed similar opinions. "It is satisfactory to be able to report the continuance of friendly relations between the Colonists and Natives of the

Some time after the termination of the session, and when the question had been freely discussed in the Assembly, and time had been allowed for patient inquiry and calm consideration, the late Chief Justice of New Zealand published a pamphlet on the " Taranaki Question." There is, probably, no individual, not in the Colony, whose judgment on the subject is entitled to greater weight. " The name of Sir William Martin," the late Governor had not long previously informed the Secretary of State, " is never mentioned without respect either by Native or European; and his experience and intimate acquaintance with the Maories cause him to be an undisputed authority in everything relating

Province. That such relations have been maintained during the past eventful year is owing, under Providence, in a great degree to the mutual confidence which twenty years of friendly intercourse have established, but still more to the part which your representatives took in the session of the General Assembly, in insisting on that investigation into the title of the disputed land which now, after repeated refusals to grant it, and after virtual military defeat, the Governor has himself proffered in the terms of peace proposed by him to the insurgents. The conduct of your representatives on that occasion removed from the minds of the Natives suspicions of the intentions of the Colonists towards them, allayed the alarm and irritation which the unjust seizure of the Waitara land had provoked, and was, I do firmly believe, the means of averting from this province, calamities greater than that which has well nigh blotted out its unfortunate neighbour from the map of New Zealand."

to them." The pamphlet itself was admitted by those whose policy it impugns to be "the fullest, the calmest, and the most able exposition of the views of those who condemn the Taranaki war." " No right of a British subject," says Sir William Martin, " is more clear or more precious that this; that the Executive Government shall not use the force at its command to oust any man from his land, or deprive him of any right which be claims, until the question between the Crown and the subject has been heard and determined by some competent tribunal— some tribunal perfectly independent of the Government, wielding the powers of a court of justice, and subject to the same checks and safeguards. This is a fundamental principle of our English Government; not only of our English Constitution, but, of necessity, a fundamental rule of all free and constitutional Governments everywhere. For, without it, the subject has no security against the aggressions of the Government. If the Government can decide the matter in its own way, and through its own dependent agents, and then take what it claims, the subject is at the mercy of the Government."

* * * At the Waitara, for the first time, a new

plan was adopted. The Governor, in his capacity of land buyer, was now to use against subjects of the Crown the force which is at his disposal as Governor and Commander-in-Chief. If this new principle was to be adopted, a new practice also became necessary. Those subjects of the Queen against whom force was to be used had a right to the protection of the Queen's Courts before force was resorted to. It is not lawful for the Executive Government to use force, in a purely civil question, without the authority of a competent judicial tribunal. In this case no such authority has been obtained, no such tribunal has been resorted to. The Government thus undertook to obtain possession of the disputed land by force, to awe the opponents into submission by a display of military force. We, the English subjects of the Queen, dislike nothing so much as being intimidated into the relinquishment of a right. Why should a Maori dislike it less? On the contrary, the pride and passion of the race, the patriotism of each clan, have always centred on this point. To fight for their land, to resist encroachment even to the death, this has been their point of honour. A Chief, who should yield to intimidation in such a case, would be degraded in the eyes of the people. The one question to be asked was this:—Was it lawful for the Government, under the circumstances, to take possession of the land by armed force? There could be only one answer,—it was not lawful."

So grave a condemnation of the proceedings of the local authorities, coming from so competent an authority as the late Chief Justice of the Colony, was sufficient to raise a serious doubt as to the justice of the war; and it is not surprising that the promoters of it were provoked to take the somewhat unusual course of publishing an official reply. In the voluminous body of "Notes" bearing the title, in the first issue, of "Notes by the Governor on Sir William Martin's pamphlet," nearly twelve months after the public had been officially and positively told that "Te Teira's title had been carefully investigated and found to be valid, and that it was not disputed by any one," it was admitted that "the title of the settlers to part of the block is certain; the Government contends that their title to the whole is probable." Thus it would seem that there was nothing but a probability on which to rest a justification for provoking and prolonging an agrarian war. Though described in the first edition as "Notes by the Governor," the internal evidence was conclusive that they were not written by the Governor himself. The "revised copy" appeared without the Governor's name, and it would be doing Governor Browne an injustice to believe that, when he gave his sanction to the publication, he was even cognizant of its contents. He would hardly describe Sir William Martin as an object of universal and deserved respect, and as an undisputed authority on Native affairs, and immediately afterwards attempt to show that he is no authority whatever—charge him with giving a false colouring to his statements—with making use of partial and misleading quotations—with being shifty, uninformed, and untrustworthy,—suggesting answers which too often give a false colouring to the subject under discussion, and which do not tend *to make the Maories loyal* subjects,—and immediately afterwards put forward a public notification requesting that further discussion of the subject should henceforward cease. Commenting on a passage in Sir William Martin's pamphlet, in which the late Chief Justice suggests that the "new policy" of the Government may have found favour with the Colonial public partly because it was profitable, the writer of the "Official Notes" tauntingly remarks, "The imputation on the Colonists of New Zealand of mere cupidity, which is conveyed by the sentence cited, should have been spared,"—a taunt which can hardly have been penned by the Governor, who, referring to the unoccupied land of the Natives, had recently informed the Secretary of State " that the Europeans covet these lands, and were determined to enter in and possess them, *recte si possint, si non quocunque modo;* that this determination becomes daily more apparent, and that neither law nor equity will prevent the occupation of Native lands by Europeans, when the latter are strong enough to defy both the Native owners and the Government." Nor is it probable that the late Governor, the author of so plain an imputation, should immediately afterwards have arrived at the conclusion set forth in the "Official Notes," that " the desire for the acquisition of territory springs from far deeper feelings than the mere love of acquisition or of property;"—that the Colonists, to whom he had imputed that neither law nor equity could prevent their occupation of Native land when they were strong enough to defy the Government, "see in the extension of British territory a guarantee for the extension of British law, and for the establishment of British sovereignty." But the promoters of the war now began to be seriously irritated to find the justice of their proceedings gravely called in question by competent authority; and all who opposed them were unsparingly condemned. The Chief of the Waitara, who had formerly been declared by the Officer in command of the Troops, on account of his services in the South, to be deserving of more consideration than any manifested towards him by the local authorities of Taranaki, was now described as "in all respects an essential savage, varnished over by the thinnest coating of Scripture phrases." The late Chief Justice of the Colony, who only two years previously had been acknowledged to be "an undisputed authority," was now treated in the "Official Notes" with but scant courtesy. Archdeacon Hadfield, who had not long previously been described by the Governor "as being more thoroughly acquainted with the Maories than any European in the country," was now entirely set aside as an authority; and the Archdeacon for whose "Christian character and talents, zeal and unwearied perseverance," the Governor had not long before expressed his admiration, was now alluded to with a covert sneer; while the clergy who, in 1856, were officially reported " to have done more to tranquillize the country than any other class of persons," were now denounced as little better than political firebands.

CHAPTER VII.

Military Operations.—War risked without Preparation.—Power of the Insurgents Underrated.—Repulse of the Troops at Puketekauere.—The out-Settlers driven in.—Women and Children sent to the neighbouring Provinces for safety. The Taranaki Settlement virtually destroyed.—Impracticable Character of the Taranaki Country for Military Operations.—The Insurgents keep the Field.—Embarrassing Position of the Governor.—Sudden Cessation of Hostilities.—Terms of Peace.—Difficulty of Warfare in the Bush.—Cost of the War.—Change in Public Opinion.—Waikato "King Movement."—Change of Ministry.—Sir George Grey appointed Governor.—The Colony saved from a General War.

APART from all question as to the justice of their proceedings, the local authorities incurred a serious responsibility in risking a collision with the Natives, especially in a land question, without first making adequate preparation for the safety of the settlers. It had long before been clearly pointed out by Sir George Grey, that the interval between the isolated English settlements was occupied by a formidable Native race, armed with rifles and double-barrelled guns, skilled in the use of them, addicted to war, and such good tacticians, that we had never succeeded in bringing them to a decisive encounter. It had also been pointed out, only a short time previously, by some of the Northern settlers, that "in case of an outbreak, protection cannot be afforded to those who are most exposed to danger, except by a military force strong enough to garrison every isolated farmhouse." Yet in the face of experience, and against all reasonable expectation, it was thought that a simple demonstration—the mere landing of two or three hundred soldiers on the beach at Taranaki—would intimidate the Chief of the Waitara and his people, and prevent them from offering any resistance to our occupation of the land. And with the insignificant force at that time in New Zealand, and before reinforcements could be procured either from England or the neighbouring colonies, actual hostilities were commenced; and the example set by ourselves of beginning the war by destroying the property of the Natives after driving them from the land, was speedily followed by their Southern Allies with the most ruinous consequences. It immediately became apparent that with the town to protect—having to maintain possession of the debateable land—and with the Southern Natives to keep at bay, we had enough to do, with the small force then at our command, even to hold our own.

Englishmen find it difficult to believe that any coloured race can make a stand before them in the field; and, until they have met the Maories on their own ground, our officers invariably underrate their military prowess. But in the attack on Puketekauere, both officers and men, who had only just landed in the Colony, found that they had to deal with no despicable antagonists. Armed with the rifle and the bayonet, and supported by artillery, our troops were driven from the field, to the astonishment of the insurgents themselves, by a Maori force not more than double the number of our own troops—having no artillery, without a single bayonet, and armed only with common muskets, fowling-pieces, and double-barrelled guns. During their retreat our troops were so closely pressed by the insurgents that our dead were left upon the field, and a number of the wounded also were abandoned to their fate. The day but one following, our dead were buried by the enemy, within a mile of our camp, and within range of our own guns. From that day, all who were engaged in this untoward affair were taught that, both in point of generalship, as well as on account of their energy and courage, the Maories, even in comparatively open ground, are a formidable enemy— a conviction which they carried with them unimpaired throughout the whole campaign.

Even before we involved ourselves in the conflict, it had almost become an axiom that if you would have a settlement destroyed, garrison it with Troops. General Pratt—who, on succeeding Colonel Gould in command, found, as he reported, "the settlers driven in from their farms, their cattle seized, and other property destroyed, many of their houses burnt, the enemy in the immediate vicinity round the town, an attack on it avowedly threatened, and the place crowded with women and children, whose only safety was the presence of the troops,"—was not long in discovering that he was engaged in a novel species of warfare, in an impracticable country, and against an active, daring, and formidable enemy; and that in superseding Colonel Gould, he had succeeded to a thankless office and a difficult command.

As soon as he had made provision for the safety of the settlers, who were all crowded together within the entrenched portion of the town, General Pratt commenced operations in the field. But the moving of a body of Regular Troops, with heavy guns and a long line of bullock drays laden with supplies, through a rugged country, without roads or bridges, and intersected in every direction by forest, and swamp-gullies and streams, was a difficult, expensive, and unprofitable undertaking. Whenever they were attacked, the Natives abandoned their defences as soon as they became untenable, and always succeeded in securing their retreat; and notwithstanding his exertions, the General was unable to bring them to a decisive encounter. Though he drove them from their strong-holds in every direction, and in the course of a few weeks captured and destroyed nearly thirty of their Pahs, his services were by no means gratefully acknowledged: and, like Colonel Gould, he had the mortification to be reminded that by the Maories their escape would certainly be regarded as a victory.

In urging the general Government to ignore the Tribal right, and to pursue a "vigorous policy," the Provincial authorities of Taranaki had represented that a large proportion of the Natives themselves would cordially support us, and that the remainder would, from the smallness of their number, be incapable of offering any effectual resistance. But the adherents of William King, including reinforcements from Waikato and the South, already amounted to about 1700 men; while Teira's supporters, who received rations, and a shilling a day each from the Government, never exceeded 300. Nor had they in truth the spirit of the insurgents; and finding themselves in a false position, they were for the most part unable to act with much cordiality in our cause. In addition to our 300 Native allies, the British forces now amounted to 2,300 men, but the difficulty of carrying on war either with honour or profit in a wild country, abounding with natural fastnesses, now began to dawn upon a few unprejudiced minds. The Governor now saw that, even with a body of the Queen's Troops considerably outnumbering the insurgents, unless some decisive advantage were speedily gained, the war might be continued indefinitely. Seeing, too, how disastrous the war had proved to the unfortunate settlers, the local authorities, who had incurred the responsibility of provoking it, became impatient for some unmistakeable success; and they were urgent that the General should adopt a system of guerilla warfare. "I have no doubt," wrote the Governor, "that a system of sudden, secret, and constant attacks, when and where they least expect it, will so distress the Natives in your neighbourhood, that when their allies return, both parties will be disheartened and glad to end their trouble by submission." The General, however, was of a different opinion. He had never probably seen an unencumbered Englishman stumbling over the slippery roots of a New Zealand forest in the vain attempt to keep up with the nimble footsteps of a Maori, with a load of forty pounds weight upon his back; but he had seen enough to know that if "it is by the legs, and not by the arms, victories are gained," it was in vain to attempt to distress the Maories by a system of guerilla warfare carried on on their own ground by Regular Troops, dependent upon a regular commissariat, and no match for the enemy in their local knowledge or in their power of moving through the bush; and as regards the capture of the Natives, the General reported that the attemps he had made to surprise them had convinced him of the hopelessness of all endeavours to prevent their escape from any place which they did not intend to defend.

"Pahs in the open country," also reported the Colonel commanding the Engineers, "will be invariably left on the approach of a hostile force. Capture of the Pah," he added, "may be in all cases calculated upon confidently with little loss; but capture of the defenders, with the experience already gained, will never be effected." The only course which remained for the General was to show the Natives that their strongest position could be approached, turned, and captured with little loss to the invaders: a system of tactics which proved indeed very galling to the enemy, but which, in the face of much adverse criticism, required no small amount of moral courage on the part of the General steadily to carry into effect.

The contest had now continued for upwards of eight months. At its commencement it was generally expected, even if we should be unable to put down the insurgents with a high hand and by striking a decisive blow, that a few months of active warfare would exhaust their ammunition and supplies; but excepting a few, who had had an opportunity of witnessing the difficulty of military operations in our former Maori wars, the public were entirely ignorant of the resources of the insurgents. In common with the Natives throughout the country—partly through an evasion of the law, and partly through the operation of the relaxed regulations of the Government—they had recently been abundantly supplied with arms and ammunition. Besides what had been supplied to them in contravention of the law, nearly eight thousand pounds weight of gunpowder, more than 300 double-barrelled guns, and nearly 500 single-barrelled guns, had in the short space of nine months not long previously been permitted to be sold to the Natives with the sanction of the authorities. If, as occasionally happened, lead ran short amongst them, they made use of Puriri or other hard-wood bullets; and to economize percussion-caps, they sometimes used them over and over again, pressing the broken edges together, and reloading them with the detonating matter on the tip of a vesta match. Being in possession of the country, living at free quarters, and following Napoleon's plan of making the war support itself, the insurgents were thus enabled to continue to keep the field, and, without incurring any serious loss, to give to the Troops no small amount of harassing and unprofitable occupation; and, foiled by their skilful and cautious tactics, the General had long to wait for an opportunity of meeting them on equal terms.

At the commencement of the outbreak it was declared by the Provincial authorities that the insurgents would soon be starved out, and that "shut up in the forest by an overpowering force in the open land, and harassed by irregulars in their retreats, they could hardly be supposed to have subsistence for a longer time than twelve months." But it was not the Natives, but the Troops and the settlers, who were really harassed and shut up; and so far from wanting the means of subsistence, it was reported of the Natives nearly a year after the commencement of hostilities, "that since the rebels were located at Waireka (a few miles' distance from the town), they had collected a large number of cattle and horses, which are sent from time to time to the Ngatiruanui country; that they were living in clover, that they had plenty of potatoes which were taken from the settlers' cultivations, and as much beef and mutton as they could eat." More than a year after martial law had been proclaimed, and when there was a military force in the Province of more than 3,000 men, exceeding the number of Natives in arms against us, the settlers of Taranaki addressed a Memorial to the Governor, stating "that the position of this settlement is very critical, and the results of the present system of carrying on the war most unsatisfactory. That notwithstanding the presence of a very considerable military force in this Province, it is yet unsafe for any person to venture beyond the outposts, in consequence of the country being continually overrun by small bands of marauding Natives within rifle-shot of the barracks. That within the last fortnight a large number of valuable houses belonging to the settlers have been burned, and great numbers of horses and cattle have been carried off by such marauders; and recently a most estimable settler has been waylaid and butchered. That the proximity of these bands, and the known existence of large bodies of Natives a short distance from the town, cause great uneasiness to the inhabitants, who feel that an overwhelming force might be brought against it at any moment without warning." The most sceptical were at length painfully convinced that the statement of one of the numerous writers on New Zealand, formerly regarded as humorous exaggeration, was really expressed in the language of soberness and truth; and that if military protection is to be effectual, it will be necessary to have "a sentinel for every cow, and a sergeant's guard to attend upon every labourer."*

As is frequently the case, the war was most keenly felt in its indirect effects. For a period of several months the settlers were not only concentrated in the town, but cooped up at

* Power's *New Zealand*.

night for safety within the narrow limits of the trenches—hardly exceeding thirty acres in extent—so that the town of New Plymouth, once celebrated for its salubrity, became a hot-bed of disease. On an average of several years the number of deaths in the Province did not exceed twelve or thirteen in each year; but in the year of the war, 1860, though the population had been materially diminished by emigration, the number of deaths amounted to sixty-eight; and in the course of the first four months of 1861, the mortality amounted to fifty-three. "In the town itself," wrote a correspondent at the end of April, "there is still much sickness; scarcely a day passes away without some death being recorded, and nearly the whole of our female population are dressed in deep mourning."

As may be readily imagined, the position of the Governor had for some time been most embarrassing. From the first, both the justice and the policy of the war had been gravely called in question. From an early period it was seen that the ground had been ill-chosen for a contest by regular troops; and, after a struggle protracted for upwards of a year, it was obvious that little progress had been made, and there appeared to be but little prospect of reducing the insurgents to submission. The Governor was no doubt persuaded that he was engaged in endeavouring to maintain the supremacy of the Crown; but he had already been reminded by Sir Cornewall Lewis that a policy which requires the continual presence of a large force carries its condemnation in its face; and he was now told by the Duke of Newcastle that, instead of being an Imperial question, the contest was regarded by her Majesty's Government as "peculiarly a Settlers' war," or as a "quarrel with William King;" and, finding himself involved in a protracted and fruitless contest for the attainment of an object which a large body of her Majesty's Maori subjects regarded as unjust, it is not surprising that the Governor now seized the earliest opportunity of bringing the contest to an end. Nor had the insurgents anything to gain by prolonging it. It was beginning to be apparent to them that they were unable to make an effectual stand before our troops, and that General Pratt was able surely, and with little loss, to dislodge them from any position they might attempt to defend. They were advised also by their friends that they might appeal with confidence to the justice of the Crown, but that it was in vain to defy its power; that while they were in arms, their complaints would not be listened to; and that they must first cease fighting, before their wrongs could be redressed; and after a period of great suffering to the Taranaki settlers, and after continuing for upwards of a year, the war came suddenly to an end—like all our Maori wars, however, without an agreement between the contending parties, and without any decided advantage on either side. Terms of peace were talked of and offered by both, but hostilities were allowed to cease before any conditions were finally agreed upon.

A few weeks before the termination of the war, William Thompson, a Waikato Chief, who had always prided himself on being a peace-maker, went down to Taranaki in the character of mediator, and with the view of inducing the contending parties to leave their differences to be determined by the judgment of the law. On arriving at the seat of war, he applied to General Pratt to grant a truce for three days, that he might confer with King and his allies; but as no satisfactory terms were afterwards proposed to the General, the fighting was resumed on the fourth day. A few days afterwards the head of the Native Land Purchase Department arrived from Auckland, instructed by the Governor to hear what terms the insurgents had to offer; and he had a meeting with William Thompson and about 100 of William King's Waikato allies. In the course of the conference, Thompson stated that the Waitara land was the cause of the quarrel, and that it would have been well if a conference of Chiefs had taken place before the commencement of hostilities; that the Natives did not fully comprehend the views of the Government; and that as they were an ignorant people, it was necessary that the Governor and the Europeans, who had great wisdom, should inquire into and adjust the quarrels arising between the two races. The meeting, however, broke off without any agreement having been arrived at.

At the conference which was held between William Thompson and William King, a number of the Waitara Natives, and the leading men of their Waikato and Ngatiruanui allies, were present. After an interchange of diplomatic courtesies between the two Chiefs, it was agreed by all present that the subject of dispute—the land at the Waitara, and the question of peace or the continuance of war—should be left to the decision of William Thompson; and in little more than half-a-dozen words, and with the air of brevity and decision of the head of a grand army, the Chief of Ngatiawa dismissed the allies to their respective homes, and, so far as Taranaki was concerned, almost instantly brought the contest to an end.

William Thompson. — " Waikato ! · Return home.

" Te Atiawa ! To Ngatiawa.

" Ngatiruanui ! Home.

" Let the soldiers return to New Plymouth.

" As for the Waitara, leave it for the LAW to protect."

And in obedience to his command, both the Ngatiruanuis and the Waikatos retired from the field; and the public, not knowing what had taken place behind the scenes, were astonished to see the Waikatos suddenly break up and disappear like a dissolving view. Shortly afterwards, the

Governor having heard that the Waitara Natives were willing to make peace, and having determined to treat separately with the several bodies of insurgents, proceeded to Taranaki ; but either because they could not agree as to the place of meeting, or for some other reason, William King and the Governor never met, and the Chief of the Waitara and a number of his people soon afterwards retired inland, without having come to any terms. The terms proposed by the Governor were accepted by a remnant of the Waitara Natives who remained upon the ground, and peace was hastily concluded with them. The Troops were withdrawn from the various redoubts, and marched into the town; and shortly afterwards, to the bewildered astonishment of the Taranaki settlers, three-fourths of the whole military was suddenly removed from the Province. To satisfy the unfortunate settlers—who were unable to see what advantage they were likely to obtain, after all their sufferings, from a war thus suddenly brought to an end, leaving many of their cultivated farms in the possession of the insurgents, who now claimed them by right of conquest; without indemnity for the past, security for the future, or any guarantee for the continuance of peace—the Governor was reported to have informed them that " the terms granted to the Ngatiawa were determined on with a view to simplify the issue in the present struggle; that it had been called a land quarrel, but though it arose out of a land quarrel, it was itself a question of jurisdiction; and that it was thought right by himself and his Executive Council to rid the issue of this extraneous matter at once, and that he thought the settlers would shortly see that this was right. The land-league, he believed, was broken up for ever in Taranaki ; and as the Natives, now that its pressure was gone, were desirous to sell land, all that was necessary for the consolidation of the settlement would, he had great hopes, be very soon obtained."

In the terms proposed to the Ngatiawa, or Waitara Natives, who, it was admitted by the Government, had been fighting for what they believed to be their rights, it was declared by the Governor that " the investigation of the title and the survey of the land at Waitara would be continued and completed; that the land in possession of her Majesty's forces would be divided amongst its former owners, with a title by grant from the Crown; that the plunder taken from the settlers must be restored, and that the Waitara insurgents in future must submit to the Queen and to the authority of the law." Regarding the ground of quarrel from the Governor's point of view, the terms offered by him were reasonable and moderate; and after having published a manifesto more than a year ago, declaring "that Te Teira's title had been carefully investigated, and found to be good; that it was not disputed by any one; that payment for the land had been received by Te Teira, and that the land now belonged to the Queen," the Governor showed no small amount of moral courage in declaring, at the end of a year of destructive warfare, that the investigation of the title should be continued." But, looked at from the Native point of view, the proposed terms appeared less satisfactory. The Chief of the Waitara and his people having been driven from their homes, as they believed, by lawless violence, and having taken up arms only in defence of what they believed to be their rights, regarded the conditions offered by the Governor as both one-sided and unjust.

In the conditions offered to William King's

Waikato allies, it was required that there must be from all submission to the Queen's sovereignty and to the authority of the law; from those who were in possession of plunder, restoration; and from those who had destroyed property, compensation. To the Ngatiruanuis similar terms were proposed, accompanied by a declaration that whenever the individuals charged with the grave offence of killing unarmed settlers and children should be taken, they would be brought to justice and dealt with according to our law. In the declaration addressed to the Waikato Natives accompanying the "terms of peace," they were informed by the Governor that submission to her Majesty's sovereign authority required that " rights be sought and protected through the law, and not by a man's own will and strength; that no man in the Queen's dominions is permitted to enforce rights, or redress wrong by force; but that he must appeal to the law." To this it was objected by the Natives, that as regards the Waitara it was the Governor himself who had been the law-breaker; that instead of appealing to the law, or without due inquiry, he had himself driven William King and his people from their homesteads by "his own will and strength." The

Waikato Natives were told also at the same time that "a large number of the adherents of the Native King had interfered between the Governor and other Native Tribes in matters with which they had no concern." "With reference," replied William Thompson, "to the going of the Waikatos to Taranaki, for which we are reproached by the Pakehas, hearken, and I will tell you. It was Potatou who fetched William King from Kapiti; he was brought back to Waitara, to his place. That was how the Ngatiawa returned to Taranaki. I look, therefore, at this word of yours, saying that 'it was wrong of the Waikatos to go to Taranaki.' In my opinion it was right for Waikato to go to Taranaki. Come now, think calmly. Raukitua, Tautara, and Ngatata were blood relations of the Waikatos. It is not a gratuitous interference on the part of the Waikatos. They were fetched; they were written for by Wiremu Kingi and Hapurona by letter; and that was why Te Wetine Taiporutu went to that war. * * * These were the grounds for Waikato's going, the bringing back (of William King) by Potatou, out of friendship to William. In the second place, because of their relations, Raukitua, Tautara, and Ngatata; the third, they were written for; the fourth, Potatou's word that land-selling should be made to cease. These were all the grounds of Waikato's interference. If the Governor had considered carefully, Waikato also would have considered carefully; but the Governor acted foolishly, and that was why the Waikatos went to help William King. For William King was a man who had not been tried, so that his fault might be seen in justification of inflicting severe punishment. You mock us, saying that this Island is one, and the men in it are one (united). I look at the Pakeha, who madly rushed to fight with William King. Had he been tried, his offence proved, and he had then been contumacious to the law, their interference would have been right, as his conduct would have been trampling on the law. As it is, that side (the Pakeha) has also done wrong. According to your word, that side is right; according to mine, also this side is right; but I think that side is wrong." A somewhat similar reply was made by Renata. " All that Waikato desired," he objected, "was to have an investigation; and for a long time, as far as talking could accomplish, they intervened between the combatants; and for a long time, whilst the

Governor was quarrelling with his son, the Waikato were strenuously smothering their feelings of sympathy. But when at length the war became permanent, then they arose to shield him (William King) from the weapon of him who was placed over him. Ought they to have given him up to darkness (death)? This is my custom: if my Chief is gently punishing his children, they are left to settle their own differences; but if I see him lift a deadly weapon, then I get up to interfere. If he thereupon turns round upon and kills me, it cannot be helped. That is a good kind of death in my—the Maori's—estimation."

"About the word relative to the murders," wrote William Thompson, addressing Governor Browne, "my opinion is decidedly that it was not murder. Look, Ihaia murdered Te Whaitere; he caused him to drink spirits, that the senses of Te Whaitere might leave him. He was waylaid, and died by Ihaia. That was a foul murder; you looked on, and made friends with Ihaia. That which we regard as a murder you have made naught of; and this, which is not a murder, you call one. This, I think, is wrong; for the Governor did not say to William King and the Ngatiruanui,

'Oh, do not kill those who are unarmed.' Nor did he direct that the settlers living in the town should be removed to Auckland, where there was no fighting, and there stay; for he knew that he had determined to make war at Taranaki; and he should therefore have told his unarmed people to remove out of the way; he did not do this. Had he even said to the Ngatiruanui, 'Friends, do not kill the settlers,' it would to some extent have been a little clearer." With regard to the claim for compensation, and for the restitution of plunder, we unfortunately ourselves destroyed the property of the Natives whom we had driven from their homes, and laid ourselves open to William Thompson's not unreasonable retort: " With reference to the property of which you say that we are to restore what remains,—that also I do not consider right. Hearken to what I propose with respect to that. The Governor was the cause of that. War was made on William King, and he fled from his Pah. The Pah was burnt, with fire; the place of worship was burnt, and a box containing Testaments: all was consumed in the fire; goods, clothes, blankets, shirts, trowsers, gowns, all were consumed. The cattle were eaten by the soldiers, and the horses, one hundred in number, were sold by auction by the soldiers. It was this that disquieted the heart of William King, his church being burnt with fire. Had the Governor given word not to burn his church, and to leave his goods and animals alone, he would have thought also to spare the property of the Pakeha. This was the cause of the Pakeha's property being lost (destroyed). When William King was reduced to nakedness through the work of the Governor, he said that the Governor was the cause of all these doings. They first commenced that road, and he (William King) merely followed upon it."

In the course of the struggle the Maories fairly fought their way to the good opinion of the English General, who was not slow to express his earnest hope that " this unhappy internecine war," with a " manly and high-spirited race," should be brought as soon as possible to an end. For obvious reasons the war was not popular with the military who were engaged in it; and throughout the campaign the officers in command were most inconsiderately judged. Instead of blaming their own rashness in plunging the Colony, without due preparation, into a costly war, its promoters sought to impute our disasters to the incompetency of the Officers in command, and blamed them for failing to accomplish impossibilities. But the responsibility for our failures must be shared by the great majority of the public, who have been too slow to recognize the fact, long since established beyond all doubt, that, man for man on their own ground, and in bush-fighting, the Maori is quite a match for the British soldier; that, in point of generalship, they are by no means inferior to ourselves; and that, against superior numbers, we have never yet gained a victory over them. Yet in the face of that experience we have continued to employ Regular Troops—trained to act in masses and under a system of parade discipline and on ground impracticable for the ordinary operations of Regular Troops—against the Natives of New Zealand, who are always led by experienced Chiefs to whom the art of war has been the study, the delight, and the practice of their lives; and we are then surprised at the small measure of our success, and but too ready to attribute our failures to the incompetency of the unfortunate Officer in command. In describing the difficulties of warfare in the New Zealand bush, those who have been engaged might echo the account given by General Turreau of the difficulty of carrying on a war in La Vendée. "It is assuredly a difficult task," says the revolutionary general, "to make war in the midst of such obstacles as bristle in the streets of La Vendée. You can never arrange beforehand your order of battle with the rebels (royalists); you know not on which side to fight, whether you will be attacked in flank or in rear, and what dispositions the country will permit of your making. The rebels, favoured by the accidents of nature, have tactics of their own which they understand applying to their position and local peculiarities. Assured of the superiority which their manner of fighting gives them, they only fight when they like.

* * * * *

"If you repulse their attack, the rebels seldom dispute the victory; but you gain little benefit, for they retire so rapidly that it is very difficult to overtake them in a country which hardly ever admits the employment of cavalry. They disperse, they escape across fields, hedges, and bushes, knowing all the paths and by-paths, what obstacles interfere with their line of flight, and how to avoid them. * * * * *

"In general, this war is so singular in its character, that one requires long practice to understand it. A general officer, whose education has been formed by ten campaigns on the frontier, finds himself much embarrassed in La Vendée. I appeal to all generals who have been summoned from the frontiers to this fearful La Vendée whether they had formed any idea of such a war till actually engaged in it? Whether the trained soldiers disciplined after the manner of Nassau and Frederick are as formidable opponents, or display such skill and courage, as these fierce and intrepid marksmen of the Bocage and Lourouse? I ask them if they can imagine a war more cruel and harassing to soldiers of every grade?—a war which ruins the discipline and subordination of an army, and makes the French soldier lose that invincible courage which has so often triumphed over the armies of England and Austria? I believe I have said enough to show that the chief obstacles to military operations in La Vendée arise from its natural features." After being exposed to much ignorant criticism for his careful tactics in the bush, it must have been gratifying to General Pratt to find that, in the judgment of the

Home Authorities, his operations "were well and judiciously carried out;" to receive a public acknowledgment of his services for bringing to a close "a war of a peculiar and difficult character;" and to receive the thanks of the Colonial Minister "for the valuable services which he had rendered to the Colony."*

* "Many people had thought," General Pratt is reported to have said, on referring to his New Zealand campaign, "that a New Zealand war could be brought to a speedy and rapid termination, by the striking of some decisive blow that would at once awe and paralyze the Maori. But people holding these opinions could not have read, or, if they had read, must have forgotten, the history of all former New Zealand wars. Neither could they have given a fair consideration to the impracticable nature of the country, and the warlike character, habits, and tactics of the athletic New Zealander. In a country singularly adapted for bush warfare, the plan of the Maories was never to expose themselves in 'the open,' but always to occupy such positions as were most difficult for an attacking party, which no party could approach without receiving great loss from the enemy, and from which the defenders had always a secure retreat; a retreat by which they could neither be intercepted nor surrounded. The only occasion on which the Maories departed from that cautious style of warfare, they met with a most signal and complete defeat; and he had reason to know that they were loudly censured and upbraided by their tribes for their rashness in that instance. It would have been easy enough for him to have ordered—and the brave soldiers under him would willingly have obeyed the order—a rush on these positions; but the proceeding would have been attended with heavy loss on our side, and trifling loss on the part of the enemy; and he felt satisfied that he was stating the truth, when he said that, so far from such conduct being

During the continuance of the war, the productive industry of the Province was brought entirely to a stand, and the whole European population crowded together within the narrow limits of a small portion of the town, suffered severely from sickness, anxiety, and harassing suspense. Both in men and money, and in the

calculated to bring the war to a conclusion, the effect would only have been to make the campaign prolonged and universal. Now, having such a foe to contend with, and having such a country of mountain and forest, swamp, gully, and fern, to operate in, and having with him a most excellent Commandant of Engineers, in the person of Colonel Mould, and a most excellent Staff, at the head of which was an officer now present, he determined upon attacking the enemy somewhat in his own style, and, by sap and redoubt, showing him that his strongest position could be approached, turned and captured, with little loss to the invaders. He had reason to know that this mode of proceeding on the part of the English force was inexpressibly galling to the Maories. They found themselves thus driven from position after position which they had occupied and fortified with care, without the power of inflicting any injury upon those opposed to them; until they could stand it no longer, and accordingly they made a most fierce attack on the English advanced redoubt. This gave an opportunity to Colonel Leslie and the gallant 40th the power of showing how slanderous were the statements which had been circulated against them. The result was well known. Now, he felt the most perfect confidence, that when the history of this war was written, when the whole truths came out, and when mis-statements were cleared up, full justice would be awarded to the expediency and wisdom of the course adopted, and to the patient endurance and gallantry of the English Troops."

destruction of property, the cost of the war was by no means inconsiderable. Our casualties amounted to 210; viz. 67 killed and 143 wounded, several of whom afterwards died of their wounds; and the extraordinary amount of sickness, the result of over-crowding and other causes, carried off upwards of 100 of the Taranaki settlers. The loss of life on the side of the Natives has not yet been clearly ascertained, but there is reason to believe that it amounted to about 150. In addition to the ordinary cost of the ships and troops employed, the expenses of the war paid by the Imperial Commissariat amounted at least to half a million sterling. To the Colony itself for Militia, Volunteers, relief and other expenses, the cost amounted to more than 200,000*l.* The neighbouring Province of Auckland also suffered severely from the sudden and complete check which was put to a stream of immigration which was yearly adding some thousands to the population of the Province. But it was the unfortunate settlers of Taranaki by whom the sufferings of the war were most severely felt. "Their losses," says the Memorial addressed by them to the General Assembly, "are variously estimated at from 150,000*l.* to a quarter of a million sterling. Two hundred houses have been burned; horses, cattle, and sheep have been killed or driven off; fencing has been destroyed; noxious weeds have overrun the cultivated lands, and the agricultural part of the community have been deprived of their means of subsistence." In its indirect effects, the war was still more disastrous; and it is to be feared that a feeling of antagonism has been excited between the Natives and the settlers, which will not easily be removed.

At the end of nearly a year of war, an Official Notification was published in the *New Zealand Gazette*, stating that "disaffection was spreading through the Maori population;" complaining that the "justice and legality" of the policy of the Government had been impugned by persons of "high authority" in various parts of the Colony; and warning the Colonists that an Englishman's privilege of freedom of speech could not any longer be exercised without danger to the State; and a body of Englishmen conscientiously believing that a portion of her Majesty's own subjects were being "unjustly and illegally" treated, were officially requested to remain silent, and to abstain from publicly criticising or censuring the conduct of the Executive until their policy should have received its final condemnation. It is no doubt possible that a people, through misgovernment or by the mismanagement of their Rulers, may be brought into such a condition that the authorities may honestly believe that even the truth may not be spoken without danger to the public safety. But, as has been said of a policy which requires the continual presence of a large force, a policy which requires the silence of conscientious men of high authority carries its condemnation on its face.

But during the progress of the contest, public opinion underwent a material change. So long as the merits of the case were imperfectly understood, it was reasonable that the public should believe that the Local Authorities had exercised a sound discretion in enforcing the purchase of the land, and at the outset, the supporters of the war formed a large majority. Many of them had been taught to believe that the land had been fairly purchased; that William King was a lawless disturber of the public peace, and that in opposing the Governor and his Ministers, he had been guilty of actual rebellion. Others thought that even if the Governor had been wrong, it would be unbecoming to recede; and that as we had entered into the struggle, the rebellious Chief must at all hazards be put down. Many rejoiced at the prospect of seeing the Maories thoroughly subdued; while others, believing that the Tribal system was about to be broken up, had confident expectations of a large extension of territory, and of abundant outlets for their flocks and herds. But, however various were the motives of the war party, they were all agreed in advocating the " vigorous prosecution " of the war. Its policy and justice, however, were warmly called in question by a small but influential minority; and the cause of the Natives was supported by them with great zeal and spirit. Those who were regarded as the best authorities on Native questions were almost unanimous in condemning the war on the ground of its injustice: many who were less clear as to the validity of the purchase believed that it was an act of madness to risk a general war by attempting to take possession of land with a doubtful or disputed title; and that so far from showing their disloyalty by opposing the war, its opponents believed that they should more worthily maintain the true dignity of the Crown and the character of the nation by preventing an act of injustice being done in the Queen's name, than by seeking to promote the triumph of a questionable cause. And for the first time in the Northern part of the Colony, the whole community were divided by a great public question. Ordinary party ties were suddenly broken, and in many instances those who for years had been opposed to one another were now ranged together on one side. After the nature of a majority, the war party were disposed to be tyrannical: adverse opinions were barely tolerated, and impatiently heard; ready evidence was given to wild stories of imaginary plots; those who ventured to express an opinion unfavourable to the war were either publicly held up to odium for giving encouragement to rebellion, or were privately denounced as disloyal to the Crown; and but that they were Englishmen, living under a free Constitution, the opponents of the war would certainly have been intimidated and put down.* But as the facts of the case gradually came to light, public opinion underwent some change; and before the war was brought to an end its justice appeared less clear, its policy was frequently called in question, and the opinion was becoming general that it had been blindly commenced, feebly conducted, and that after a fruitless waste of life and property, it had been brought to a hasty and unsatisfactory conclusion. And the Ministers who had advised the Governor to risk the war, finding that it had been productive of nothing but disastrous results, and that the Home Authorities regarded it simply as a "Settlers' war," now appeared by no means unwilling, so far as the original cause of quarrel was concerned, to bring the war at the Waitara to an end, and to hazard an imperial contest at the Waikato for the suppression of the Maori King.†

* The recent experience of America has proved that "free institutions" give no security against the most flagrant acts of tyrannical despotism.

† "Great pains have been taken to submerge the Waitara Land Question under that of the King Movement; but it must be remembered that until the declaration of war they were perfectly separate. Great stress has also been put upon the necessity of 'upholding her Majesty's supremacy.' Perhaps it will startle

But, in addition to the virtual destruction of the settlement, the war at Taranaki had cost three quarters of a million; and the settlers in other parts of the Island, with the experience of Taranaki before them, and believing that the Government were prepared to take up a new ground of quarrel in another province, and to march the Troops into the interior to enforce the submission of the Waikato Tribes, and to put down the Maori King, now became alarmed lest war might be brought to their own doors, and find them unprepared. A committee was therefore appointed by the Assembly to report upon the military defence of the Colony; and a deputation of Representatives of the Province of Wellington earnestly warned the Governor not to risk war a second time without making timely provision for the safety of the principal settlements. The Superintendent of the Province (Dr. Featherston), who was the chief spokesman, said that "they came in their capacity of Representatives of the Province of Wellington, to point out to his

the reader when I assert that among all her Majesty's Maori subjects, there is not one at this moment more loyal in disposition than Wiremu Kingi himself."—*Remarks, &c. by G. Clarke, late Chief Protector of Aborigines.*

Excellency how utterly inadequate the forces at present stationed there would be to afford almost any protection in the event of a rising among the Natives. They regretted to be obliged to inform his Excellency that though peace had hitherto been preserved, and that though some considerable time after the commencement of the war at Taranaki there was every reason to believe that the great bulk of the Natives would continue loyal and well-affected; yet, owing to various causes, a feeling of intense distrust of the Government had within the last few weeks taken possession of the Native mind; large numbers were giving in their adhesion to the "King movement," and in fact almost the whole Native population might be said to be preparing for a war which they deemed inevitable. What the Natives said was simply this, that as long as the war was confined to Taranaki, they looked upon it as a dispute between the Governor and William King about land, which would be settled sooner or later without their being dragged into a quarrel; but that if the war was carried by the Government into other parts they could and would only regard it as a proof of the determination of the Government to attack and destroy them in detail, and that they would be forced to take part in the war. Even the most loyal Chiefs—those who had proved themselves staunch allies of the Government—declared that if war was carried into the Waikato country it would be the signal for a general rising; they might not themselves join, but their tribes would make common cause with the Waikatos. Since they had been in Auckland they (the members) had seen and heard enough to satisfy them that there *was a strong probability* of military operations being undertaken in the Waikato country.

The Governor, in a semi-official publication, is reported to have informed the deputation that 20,000 soldiers could not protect all the out-settlers; that in the event of an attack they would have to take refuge in the centres of population — build block-houses as the settlers at Taranaki had done, and defend them: and that war carried on in a country where wealth and property are scattered broadcast must be attended with great loss and very serious consequences. That the terms he had proposed to the Waikatos he intended should be insisted on; and that he believed at the first shot that was fired in the Waikato there would be a general rising of the Tribes connected with the King Movement in the several Provinces. But the Government who had already burdened the Colony with a heavy debt for a disastrous war were prevented from provoking a second war on a still more costly scale, being shortly afterwards defeated on a vote of want of confidence, and displaced by a Ministry desirous of avoiding a renewal of the war. The Home Authorities also being satisfied at length that " little effect had really been produced by the military operations at Taranaki," and that disaffection was spreading through the country, and feeling that no expedient should be left untried to arrest the growing evil, determined for the second time to avail themselves of the peculiar qualifications and experience of Sir George Grey; and commissioned him to proceed at once to New Zealand to take the place of Governor Browne, and the Colony was opportunely relieved from the imminent risk of a still more general war.*

* *" Downing Street*, 25th *May*, 1861.
" SIR,—I have perused with much anxiety the intelligence respecting the progress of the Native war, which is contained in your despatches, recently arrived.

"I cannot but perceive that, in spite of some symptoms of a desire on the part of the Natives for the restoration of peace, little effect has really been produced hitherto by the military operations at Taranaki; and that, notwithstanding all the efforts of yourself and your advisers, the disaffection of the Maories is extending itself to those Tribes whose amity, or, at least, whose neutrality, has hitherto been hoped for, and is assuming a more organized form, and a more definite object.

"I am far indeed from ascribing this untoward course of events to those who are responsible for the conduct of affairs in New Zealand. On the contrary, I recognize with pleasure the sound and impartial judgment, the integrity, intelligence, and anxiety for the public good, which have characterized your government of the Colony for nearly six years. The present conjuncture, however, renders it necessary for her Majesty's Government to leave no expedient untried which is calculated to arrest the course of events now unhappily so unpromising; and, at the same time, to provide for the future difficulties, which there is only too much reason to anticipate, even if the war should happily be soon brought to a conclusion.

"Having regard, therefore, to the peculiar qualifications and experience of Sir George Grey, now governing the Cape of Good Hope, I have felt that I should be neglecting a chance of averting a more general and disastrous war if I omitted to avail myself of the remarkable authority which will attach to his name and character as Governor of New Zealand.

"I trust, therefore, that you will not feel it as any slight on yourself that I should have determined to place the Government of the Islands in his hands at a moment when your own term of office has all but expired, and you would have no opportunity of providing against those future difficulties to which I have referred. I hope that, in doing so, I shall not deprive the Crown for any long period of the advantage of your services."

CHAPTER VIII.

Impolicy of risking a War at Taranaki.—Policy of the Government as officially explained. — Hostilities: by whom commenced.—The Natives blamed for not appealing to the Law.—Result of the War.—Future Policy.

THE more the subject is considered the more remarkable appears to have been the blindness of the authorities in plunging the Colony into war. Unless the character of the New Zealanders has been entirely misrepresented, it would not have been consistent with the maintenance of his position for a Maori Chief to submit without resistance to be driven with his people from the land they were occupying, and to see their claims openly disregarded. Nor, looking to the character of the Chief of the Waitara, his power and influence, and seeing that in the presence of the assembled people he had distinctly declared that Waitara was in his hands, and that he would not give it up; that he had formally, and in writing, declared that the land belonged to the whole of the people, and that it would not be given up, never until he died—was it probable that he would quietly acquiesce in being driven from the land? Nor is it easy to see how the proceedings of the authorities, in taking possession of land by military force before it was ascertained that all who had the power to sell were willing to sell, were considered to be necessary for the maintenance of the Queen's supremacy. Looking to the nature of the Taranaki country—to the amount of force available for the purpose—and to the jealousy with which the Natives regard any infringement of their territorial rights, it is certain that neither the time, the place, nor the occasion was well chosen for a collision with the Natives, either with a view to prove the justice of our rule—to establish the prestige of our power—or to maintain the supremacy of the Crown.

The grounds on which the Local Executive justified their proceedings have been frequently explained. In his speech to the General Assembly in opening the session of 1860, after referring to the attempt of William King to prevent the sale of the Waitara, it was declared by the late Governor, that he "felt it to be his duty to repel this assumption of an authority inconsistent alike with the maintenance of the Queen's sovereignty and the rights of the proprietors of the land in question.' In opening the following Session, he informed the Assembly that, "in the policy which he had pursued with reference to the affairs of Taranaki, his object from the first had been to secure peace by putting an end to the constantly recurring land feuds which for years had maintained barbarism amongst them." In afterwards offering terms of peace to the Waitara Natives (April, 1861), he declared that he did not use force for the acquisition of land, but for the vindication of the law and for the protection of her Majesty's Native subjects in the exercise of their just rights. In the exposition of his motives, given by him immediately after the event, he informed her Majesty's Ministers that "he had insisted on this comparatively worthless purchase, because if he had admitted the right of a Chief to interfere between him (the Governor) and the lawful proprietors of the soil, he should soon have found further acquisitions of territory impossible." He was informed, and he doubtless believed, that the Chief of the Waitara had no legitimate title to a voice as to the disposal of the land in question. He declared that any recognition of such a power as that assumed by William King would be unjust to both races, because it would be the means of keeping millions of acres of waste land out of cultivation. He doubtless expected, too, that if the purchase were completed, it would probably lead to the acquisition of all the land south of the Waitara River, which was essentially necessary for the consolidation of the Province, as well as for the use of the settlers. Believing, too, that the Chief of the Waitara would not venture to maintain his assumed right, and that by making a mere demonstration he should be able to confer a solid benefit on the Colony, the late Governor, supported by the advice of his Ministers, hastily, and without adequate preparation, proceeded to dispossess the actual occupants of the land by military force. A somewhat similar proceeding in Cook's Straits, nearly twenty years ago, drew from the then Colonial Minister the most grave condemnation. In that case, a civic magistrate, armed with a regular warrant for the apprehension of Te Rauparaha, and supported by a numerous body of armed followers, finding that Chief unwilling to surrender himself, ordered his party to advance. Shots were fired by both sides, and many valuable lives were sacrificed. "So manifestly illegal, unjust, and unwise," said Lord Derby, "were the martial array, and the command to advance, that I fear the authors of that order must be held responsible for all that followed in natural and immediate sequence upon it. I know not how to devolve that responsibility upon the Natives; they exercised the rights of self-defence and of mutual protection against an imminent, overwhelming, and deadly danger. Revolting to our feelings as Christians, and to our opinions as members of a civilized state, as was the ultimate massacre, it is impossible to deny to our savage antagonists the benefit of the apology which is to be urged in their behalf. They who provoke an indefensible warfare with barbarous tribes are hardly entitled to complain of the barbarities inseparable from such contests."

An attempt was made to fix upon the Natives the responsibility of commencing the war; but long before hostilities commenced it appears to have been determined that William King's claim to a voice in the disposal of the Waitara should be ignored, and that his opposition, if necessary, should be overborne by force; and the Governor's advisers decided that "the case in question was as favourable a one of its class as could have been selected," that the issue had been carefully chosen, and that the occasion had arisen, on which it had become necessary to support the Governor's authority by military force." If their intentions had been made known to the public, it is probable that representatives would have been brought forward sufficient to raise a doubt as to both the justice and the policy of such a proceeding, and to prevent Ministers from carrying it into execution. But wishing to avoid any public discussion of the subject, their design was purposely kept secret. As to the interruption of the survey, it was managed in the least objectionable way possible; and yet, almost immediately afterwards, no breach of the peace having in the meantime taken place, the public were informed by a proclamation of martial law that "active military operations were about to be undertaken by the Queen's forces against Natives in the Province of Taranaki," and the Natives were at the same time informed by a proclamation in the Maori language,* that the law

* "With respect to the translation of the proclamation of martial law at Taranaki into Maori, a grievous error was committed,

of fighting was about to commence, and that until further notice, fighting was to be the order of the day; the Troops were marched out in martial array to occupy the disputed block of land; and the land which the Chief of the Waitara and his people had occupied for years was taken possession of by the soldiers, by whom the first shot was fired. Under these circumstances it is difficult to understand, except on the principle that " he who *returns* the first blow begins the fray," how it could be maintained that the war was commenced by William King.

As the Chief of the Waitara directly appealed to the fountain of justice in the Colony—claiming the land for the whole of his people, declaring at the same time that he was anxious for the preservation of peace, it is not easy to see, in the absence of any constitutional tribunal, and failing his appeal to the representative of the Crown, what remedy was open to the Waitara Natives for the protection of their interests and

the meaning of that proclamation having been entirely changed by the translator. A New Zealander would understand it thus: ' Arm yourselves for the battle; and we will fight it out.' It is, in fact, an invitation to take up arms."—*George Clarke, formerly Protector of Aborigines.*

for vindication of their rights. It is true that, after martial law had been proclaimed, and after the Governor had determined to resist by force of arms, the Chief of Waitara was invited to come into the English settlement; and he has been blamed for not complying with the Governor's invitation. But it would seem that some time previously he expressed a strong apprehension that there was an intention on the part of the Government to seize him like Te Rauparaha. It can hardly be looked upon, therefore, as culpable contumacy on the part of that Chief to decline to come into the settlement, after it had been declared in the name of the Governor that the Queen's Troops were about to commence active military operations against the Natives of the district. Two facts, however, have since been made clear with respect to him, that long before any anti-land-selling league had been heard of in the country he had declared his determination not to give up the Waitara, and that he had no connection with the so-called "King movement," until after martial law had been proclaimed.

It has been allowed by the promoters of the war, that the Chief of the Waitara and his people believed that they were fighting for their rights; but they have been blamed for taking up arms, instead of appealing to the law; yet it does not appear what tribunal or what legal remedy was open to them by which their claims could be judicially determined, and legally enforced. By an Act of the local Legislature, it had been declared that no court of law or equity in the Colony has any cognizance of any question affecting the title or right to or over Native lands. "The position of the Native race," said Chief Justice Amey, in addressing the Legislative Council, "is a most extraordinary and anomalous one. They are practically without rights, for they have lately been pronounced to be without a remedy.* After

---

* In answer to the question afterwards submitted to them by the Governor of the Colony, whether an efficient Court could be established for disposing of questions relating to land over which the Native title had not been extinguished, the Judges of the Supreme Court gave an opinion, of which the following is an extract:—

"By treating the latter in the largest and most general way, we feel justified in suggesting that a competent tribunal might be established by the formation of a Land Jury, selected by lot or otherwise from members of the various Tribes in previously defined districts, nominated by such Tribes as competent to act in that capacity, to be presided over by a European Officer or Commissioner (not being an agent of the Crown for the purchase of land), conversant with the Maori language, and assisted, if

twenty years of government, during which period the Colony has been advancing in wealth and legislation, all that legislation has profited, is little; he is practically beyond the protection of the laws.

" And who are this people ? Politically they are a people to whom twenty years ago the Queen guaranteed all the rights and privileges of British subjects, and this Colony has been enriched and our own Government established on the faith of that guarantee. In numbers they are about one-half of her Majesty's subjects in these islands, far more than half of the population, for whose benefit the Government of this Northern Island has been supposed to be administered. True also, they have been christianized (thanks to the self-denying zeal of the missionary); as a people they have shown themselves teachable, capable of civilization, easily convinced by reason and argument, no longer generally disposed to quarrel among them-

necessary, by a Native Assessor, and whose duty it should be merely to propound the questions for the decision of the Jury, to record their verdicts, and to administer oaths to witnesses.

" (Signed)   GEORGE ALFRED AMEY, Chief Justice.
" ALEX. J. JOHNSTON.
" HENRY B. GRESSON.

selves, not factious nor unruly: I accept the memorandum appended to these papers as an index of their domiciliary condition. It shows that they possess little to tempt the cupidity of the unscrupulous; but they do possess that one ewe lamb, their land. It is this which they love and cherish. For this they have fought and bled, and at Taranaki we now find they will still fight and bleed again and again; and yet it is in respect of this darling object of their patriotism, their property, their all, that now after twenty years of successive governments, from the direct government of the Crown to the present responsible Government under our Constitution Act, the Attorney General of England is constrained to tell them their rights can neither be recognized, ascertained, nor regulated by English laws. Their property is without the pale of the jurisdiction of the Queen's Court."

For "Indian" read "New Zealand," and for "Pondiac" read "William King," and the history of our war with the North American Indians a century ago might serve to describe the Taranaki war. "The Indian war was now drawing to a close, after occasioning great disquiet, boundless expense, and some bloodshed; even when we had the advantage which our tactics and artillery in some instances gave, it was a warfare of the most precarious and perplexing kind. It was something like hunting in a forest at best, could you but have supposed the animals you pursued armed with missile weapons, and ever ready to start out of some unlooked-for place. * * * We said, however, that we conquered Pondiac— at which no doubt he smiled; for the truth of the matter was, the conduct of this war resembled a protracted game of chess. He was as little able to take our forts without cannon, as we were able, without the feet, the eyes, and the instinctive sagacity of Indians, to trace them to their retreats. After delighting ourselves for a while with the manner in which we were to punish Pondiac's presumption, could we but once catch him, all ended in our making a treaty, very honourable for him, and not very disadvantageous to ourselves. We gave both presents and promises, and Pondiac gave permission to the mothers of those children who had been taken away from the frontier settlements, to receive them back again on condition of delivering up the Indian prisoners."* Our recent experience has proved that war in New Zealand, when it can be avoided, is not only a crime but a blunder. A warlike and high-spirited race like the New Zealanders may be civilized, or they may possibly be exterminated; but they can hardly be subdued. In the art of war they are quite equal to ourselves; in knowledge of the country they have the advantage over us; they have comparatively little to lose, and they can always find subsistence on the sheep and cattle of the settlers: unencumbered, too, with baggage, and independent of a regular commissariat, they can move freely and with great rapidity, and can always choose when and where to make a stand; and in the neighbouring forests they are sure in case of need of finding a secure retreat. If the Maories had been a civilized people and we had been the barbarians; if they had a rich capital to be plundered, or a Summer Palace to be sacked, we might have gone to war with them with a reasonable prospect of success; but being ourselves the owners of valuable property, and having a hundred defenceless homesteads open to attack, the

* *Memoirs of an American Lady.*

local authorities, when they declared war against the Natives of Taranaki, engaged in a ruinous undertaking. By the Chief of the Waitara and his immediate followers, the war was conducted with as much high-spirited generosity and forbearance as the most civilized nation would have shown;* but by murder, pillage, and the wanton destruction of property, the Natives from the south brought discredit on his cause. In destroying the habitations of the people, in setting fire to their corn-stacks, in breaking up their flour-mills, and in opening their potato stores to be devoured by the pigs, we ourselves also either set or followed a barbarous example.

Seeing that he was obliged to act under a Constitution which was "framed in forgetfulness of the large Native Tribes within the dominions to which it was intended to apply," the late Governor was placed in a trying and anomalous position. To the heavily-burdened taxpayers of Great

---

* "William King," said the Governor, in an official notification contrasting his conduct with the Ngatiruannis, "William King is a Chief, and he did not make war on the unarmed and the helpless. He said his quarrel was with the Governor and the soldiers, and if the settlers did not molest him, he should not molest them."

Britain, who have been called upon to pay half a million sterling for a fruitless attempt to vindicate his authority, the policy pursued by him may not be satisfactory; but to the Colonists his answer is complete: the authorities of Taranaki urged him to try a new system to obtain land at the Waitara: his Ministers advised him to have recourse to military force: a majority in both Houses of the Assembly expressed their approval of his policy; and from all parts of the Colony he received assurances of sympathy and support. He no doubt formed a mistaken estimate of the probable consequences of his own acts, but he is fairly entitled to the consideration claimed by Lord Grey in favour of the Governors of distant Colonies, that "in times of civil commotion they are placed in situations of so much difficulty and responsibility, that every generous mind will be disposed to put the best construction on their conduct, and to believe, until the contrary is clearly proved, that they have acted to the best of their judgment and ability."

But if the Taranaki war has been disastrous, it has not been without some good result; it has shown the importance to the general interests of the Colony of the good government of the Native race; it has shown that the interests of the two races are inseparable; that the successful colonization of the country is possible only so long as peaceable relations are maintained between them; and that the best guarantee for the preservation of peace consists not so much in the number of our forces as in the justice of our rule. What provision shall be made for securing the fulfilment of the obligations we have contracted in favour of the Natives—what measures should be taken for promoting peace, order, and good government amongst them—to whom may the administration of Native affairs be most advantageously entrusted—are questions of which Governor Grey is now engaged in attempting a solution. Opinions no doubt differ as to the particular measures to be adopted, but all are agreed that whatever they may be, it is essential to their success that they should have the cordial co-operation of the Colonial Parliament.

It is impossible, however, to win the willing obedience of a free people simply by the sword. By a ruinous sacrifice of property, by a large expenditure of money, and after a protracted period of miserable warfare, we should no doubt be able to decimate the Maori race; but instead of rendering the remainder good subjects of the Crown, we should probably reduce them to the condition of a sullen, discontented, and dangerous class, whom it would then be impossible to govern excepting by the sword. But it would be a poor triumph for a powerful nation like Great Britain to crush by the sword a few Native Tribes, just rising out of barbarism, who, relying on our justice and good faith, have confidingly placed themselves within our power; it would be but little to our credit as a colonizing people, if we shall be unable to govern excepting by the sword a conquered remnant of the Maori race. But be just, and, as Sir W. Martin has observed, "you may easily govern the Maories." Be just, and a moderate force will suffice. Be unjust, and a force far larger than England can spare will not suffice. Force is good if subordinate to justice, but it is a sorry substitute for it. The Maori is not to be intimidated; but, like all other human creatures, he is to be influenced through his sense of fair dealing and of benefit received; he is governed by the same motives and led by the same inducements, as other men. Let the Maories be practically taught that our laws are better than their laws, and that our rule is better than their own; let them understand at the same time that in their relations with each other, and so far as is consistent with the supreme authority of the Crown, and with the general interest of the Colony, they may, if they desire it, govern themselves by themselves, and that we will aid them both with money and with men—we shall then have endeavoured to fulfil the obligations we have undertaken in their favour, and have taken at the same time the most reasonable means of securing their willing allegiance, and of removing any desire they may entertain for the maintenance of a separate nationality, independent of the Crown. Here, then, "in New Zealand our nation has engaged in an enterprise most difficult, yet also most noble and worthy of England. We have undertaken to acquire these Islands for the Crown and for our race, without violence and without fraud, and so that the Native people, instead of being destroyed, should be protected and civilized. We have covenanted with these people, and assured to them the full privileges of subjects of the Crown. To this undertaking the faith of the nation is pledged. By these means we secured a peaceable entrance for the Queen's authority into the country, and have in consequence gradually gained a firm hold upon it. The compact is binding irrevocably. We cannot repudiate it so long as we retain the benefit which we obtained by it.*

* "The Taranaki Question."—*Sir William Martin.*

THE END.

www.ingramcontent.com/pod-product-compliance
Lightning Source LLC
Chambersburg PA
CBHW021729220426
43662CB00008B/768